LEARNING TO RELAX

When you want to practise relaxing, you should feel nice and comfortable. Loosen ties and belts; kick your shoes off. Choose a quiet, warm room where you will not be interrupted Sit in a comfortable chair or, better still, lie down. Close your eyes and concentrate on the feelings of your body. Notice how you are breathing and where body tensions are.

BREATHING

Start to breathe slowly and deeply, expanding your abdomen as you breathe in, till your lungs are filled right to the top. Hold for several seconds, then exhale slowly, relaxing your rib cage and stomach, and emptying your lungs completely. Do not strain; it will become easier.

RELAXATION

After you've established a regular slow breathing pattern start the following sequence.

1. Curl your toes hard and press your feet down. Tense up on an in-breath, hold for ten seconds while keeping your muscles tense, then relax and breathe out (at the same time).

2. Press your heelds down and bend your feet up. Tense up on an in-breath, hold for ten seconds, relax on an out breath, as before.

3. Tense up your calf muscles. Tense up on an in-breath hold for ten seconds; relax on an out breath

4. Tense your thigh muscles, straightening your knees and making your legs stiff. Tense up on an in breath, hold for ten seconds; relax on an out-breath.

5. Make your buttocks tight. Tense up on an in breath, hold for ten seconds; relax on an out breath.

6./

6. Tense your stomach as if to receive a punch. Tense on an in-breath, hold for ten seconds; relax on an out-breath.

7. Bend your elbows and tense your arm muscles on an in-breath, hold for ten seconds; relax on an out-breath.

8. Hunch shoulders and press your head back into the cushion, mattress or carpet. Tense up on an in-breath, hold for ten seconds; relax on an out-breath.

9. Clench your jaws, frown and screw up your eyes tightly. Tense up on an in-breath, hold for ten seconds; relax on an out-breath.

10. Now tense all your muscles together on an in-breath hold for ten seconds; relax on an out-breath.

Remember to breathe deeply and slowly and be aware when you relax of the feeling of well-being and heaviness spreading throughout your whole body.

Now, still breathing slowly and deeply, image a bright yellow rose against a white background. Try to "see" the flower as clearly as possible, concentrating for 30 seconds. Breathe as before. Then tell yourself that when you open your eyes you will be perfectly relaxed and alert. Count to tend and open your eyes.

New Food

New Food

HELENE HODGE

Foreword by Pat Phoenix

COLUMBUS BOOKS
LONDON

For Stephen,
without whose support and encouragement
this book would not have been written

A note on quantities

This is not a book about meat-and-two-veg meals. 'New Food' meals are more like Indian or Chinese meals, in that the number of people a dish will serve depends on what other dishes are to be served in the context of that meal. What serves two people for supper on one night might easily form part of a meal with other dishes when you are entertaining. Overall, the aim should be to stop thinking in terms of vegetable dishes to accompany some sort of main dish and start thinking of carbohydrates in proper balance to proteins – and proteins in proper balance to one another. However, in order to provide some form of quick, at-a-glance guide to serving quantities indications have been given for the vast majority of recipes.

Copyright © 1985 Helene Hodge
Colour photographs by Anthony Blake

First published in Great Britain in 1985 by
Columbus Books
Devonshire House, 29 Elmfield Road, Bromley, Kent BR1 1LT

British Library Cataloguing in Publication Data
Hodge, Helene
    New food: delicious low-salt, low-cholesterol, low-sugar meals.
    1. Cookery (Natural foods)
    I. Title
    641.5'637   TX741

Printed and bound by
Butler and Tanner Ltd, Frome, Somerset

ISBN 0 86287 183 2

Contents

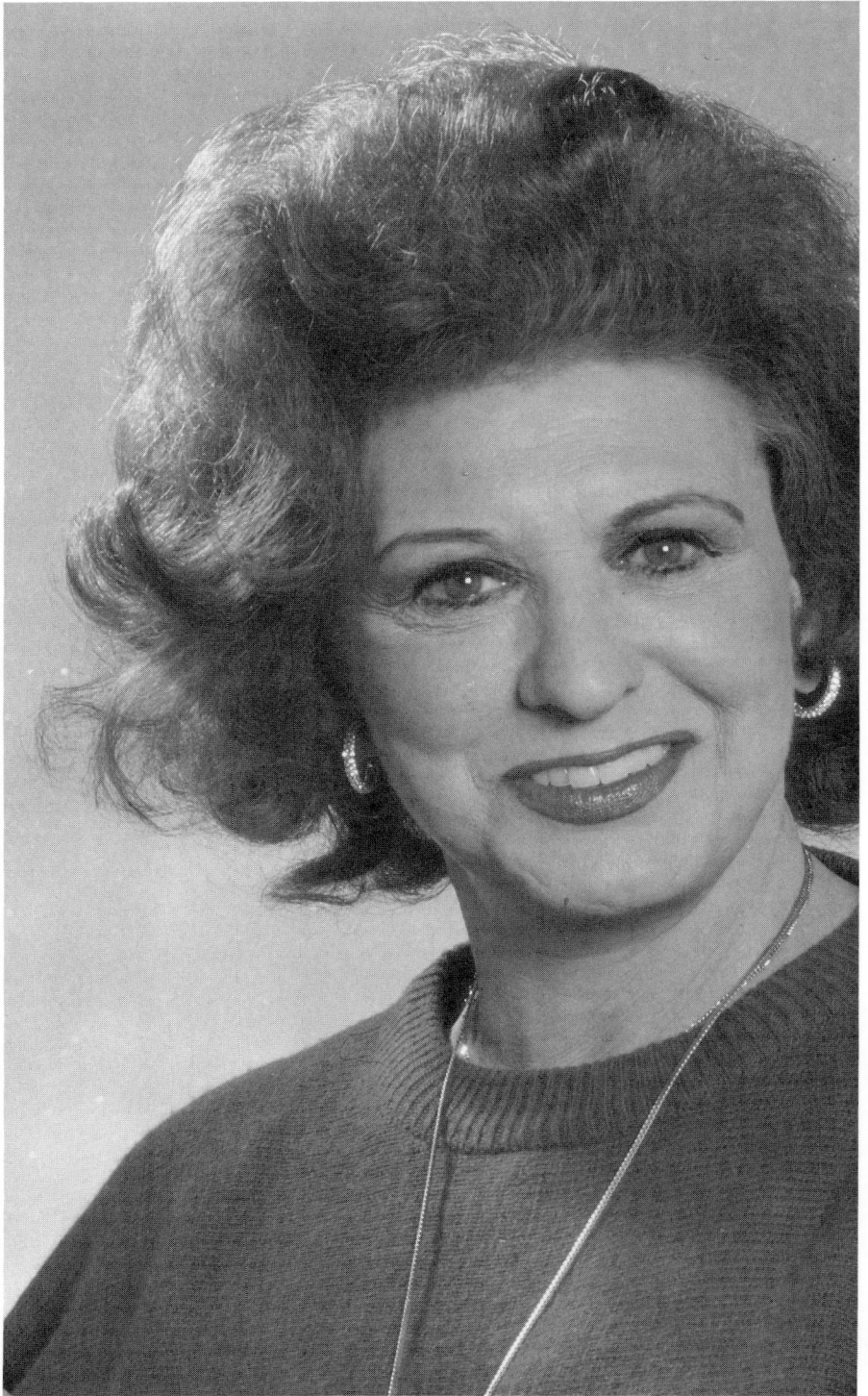

Foreword

I learnt very early in my career that the most essential equipment any actress could have was not looks, glamour or star-spangled publicity but health and stamina.

The life of a young actress was hard: hours of study into the early mornings, cold lodgings, overheated theatres, travel in all weathers, bad – and very often insufficient – food.

At thirty I learnt that I had a lung condition which was to recur throughout my life. The hard work plus the lung condition did not seem conducive to a long career.

It was some years – about sixteen, to be precise – before I discovered a better way of living.

I was on my knees, hitting the deck, head in hands and totally exhausted, when my best friend Keith Pollitt arrived on the scene, rather like a fairy godmother and right on cue. He introduced me to a new, healthier way of living which began with a course of herbal food supplement. I became deeply interested in herbs and herbal cures – and most important, healthy eating.

It is difficult, in my profession, to get the best food all the time. Everything I do is done on the run. I travel extensively, dashing from one date to another, sometimes *having* to snatch at junk foods because there is nothing else available at the time. This can lead to indigestion and a few extra rolls of fat which I can well do without . . . not to mention a guilty conscience.

It is always a struggle to keep my weight at a reasonable level. Crash diets (and I've tried them all) are useless to me: I need all the energy I can muster, and that is much more than the average person requires.

In the last year, I have done more travelling and dashing about than I have ever done in my life, and some of my healthy principles have, I'm afraid, not always been maintained. I became nervy, fraught, irritable and just plain hell to live with. And what was even worse, the lung condition reappeared – at sixty years of age. Working full out and under pressure every single minute, I cannot afford to become run down, or in any way under par.

So I have gone back to my former healthy eating regime, in the nick of time. One big problem for me, of course, is that I am hardly ever at home to arrange menus or organize meals. The gradely folk who look after Tony and myself were scratching their heads to find different, healthy ways of feeding us. Boredom had set in on the food front.

Wholemeal bread, fresh vegetables and baked apples were becoming boring, and our people were running out of ideas. And what about entertaining? We could run along on that sort of a diet, but you can't give it to your guests – or can you?

Then I was shown a draft copy of *New Food*. I became so excited at the recipes I dropped pages all over the floor! I read it all out of order, but nevertheless I was delighted at what I read. Here at last was healthy food that was also *EXCITING*! We couldn't wait to try out the menus . . . the delicious 'poulet parcels', creamy pancake roll, Chinese lettuce baskets – these were among the first we tried, all totally delicious.

I really believe that Helene Hodge has written a book of some importance. For me she has taken the boredom out of what may have been healthy but was becoming rather monotonous eating.

The chapter on protein power was a re-education. Imagine – we need only 37 grams of protein a day – and less than 2 lb of spinach could provide all our daily needs (I can eat 2 lb of spinach in a salad). But apart from all that, the recipes are such that they can really tickle my jaded palate, without giving me the guilty fear that I have gorged myself on fatty, unhealthy foods.

So now I really believe I have myself organized. I am feeling fit and healthy again and I would recommend this book to all those with hectic, busy lives. Keeping well is the first essential.

Good luck, keep well – and healthy eating.

Pat Phoenix

Introducing the 'new food'

Eating can be a risky business. As new medical evidence emerges it is becoming increasingly apparent that eating the wrong food can cause lasting damage to your health. Eating the right kind of food is, on the other hand, a form of life insurance.

Slowly but surely attitudes towards diet are changing. More people are becoming aware of the need to reduce their intake of fat, sugar and salt and to increase the amount of fibre in their diet. People are gradually waking up to the hazards of eating too many processed and refined foods. But many people are not clear how to break away from these old eating habits – and no one wants to be labelled a health-food crank.

This book attempts to show a way forward. Drawing on the latest research carried out in the field of nutrition, it explains which are the best foods to eat for health's sake and how to use them imaginatively in a wide range of recipes. Throughout, the emphasis is on the positive value of natural foods. The recipes reflect this and prove that food does not have to be loaded with sugar, salt and fat to be delicious. Many of the recipes have been specially devised so that old favourites can be cooked using 'new' ingredients in place of more traditional ones, and so given a healthier slant. Others present ingredients in exciting, possibly unfamiliar, combinations that will open up a new world of taste experience. The recipes range from simple, everyday dishes to others that would grace any dinner-party menu, and prove that meals based on 'healthy' foods can be every bit as impressive as the more traditional ones.

Positive health

Health, as defined by the World Health Organization, is a state of complete physical, mental and social well-being – not simply the absence of disease or infirmity. While this may be an ambitious requirement, it is surely something worth trying to achieve. It is also what this book is all about.

The increasing interest in health has created a greater awareness of diet. The media coverage currently given to self-help, exercise and alternative therapies has made people realize that diet is the first step in their search for self-improvement.

The links between smoking, cancer and coronary heart disease are well established: now medical research is further establishing the relationship between coronary heart disease and bad diet. Specifically, our intake of fat, sugar and salt has been called into question, for these foods have been shown to cause problems ranging from cholesterol build-up in the bloodstream to obesity and hypertension; in combination with other food substances, such as additives and preservatives, they can produce other diseases and also allergic reactions.

As the media coverage of health continues apace, more people are thinking about incorporating wholefoods, those foods as near their natural state as possible, into their diet in place of highly refined foods. However, for many people the problem is knowing where to start. What exactly are these wholefoods, and how are they used? How do you plan a meal containing little or no meat when meals based on the 'meat and two veg' principle have always been the norm? What are the healthier alternatives to foods that should be reduced or omitted from the diet altogether? And how do these 'new' ingredients behave in recipes?

These are among the questions that this book sets out to answer. It will also explain the significance of current research into nutrition. Each chapter deals with a different element of diet, provides a selection of tested recipes and shows practically how to use health-food substitutes for more traditional ingredients.

Perhaps a brief word on terminology would be useful before the great food debate begins, particularly the confusion over healthy eating *vis-à-vis* calories. Nutrients are the fuel that the body needs to function properly; the units in which this fuel, or heat, is expressed are calories. High-energy foods are also high in calories, and *vice versa*. (As a rough guide, fats represent about 9 calories per gram, carbohydrates about 3 per gram.) A low-calorie diet is not necessarily a healthy one: you can cut down calories in order to lose weight yet still be eating an unhealthy, because un-balanced, diet.

How 'bad' eating started

It is a sad fact, but the unhealthy trends in food consumption which are now stimulating so much media interest have been developing over the last thirty years.

In Britain, for example, these habits began as a natural reaction to war-time food rationing. During the boom period of the 'sixties an ever-increasing variety of attractive foods, including many processed 'convenience' foods, appeared in the shops. By that time, practically everyone could afford to eat the sort of food they liked best. Most people got into the habit of indulging themselves with a very rich diet, high in animal proteins, animal fat and sugar.

Starchy foods like bread and potatoes, with which people had been obliged to fill themselves up during the war, were given the cold shoulder, and bread consumption plummeted during the late 'fifties. During the austerity period meat, too, had been in short supply. Under rationing each person had been allowed about 450g (1lb) of carcass meat each week. Many of us may not eat much more than that now but we do eat a lot of other meats in convenient forms such as ready-cooked cold meats, canned meat, luncheon meat, meat pies and other meat products with a high fat content.

During the war the cheese ration stood at about 75 (3oz) a week for most people, which is 25 per cent less than the average consumption of cheese today. Milk and eggs were also rationed, and today we drink on average twice as much milk and eat four times as many eggs as we did during the war years.

Sweets and other confectionery were also rationed, to just 100g (4oz) a week per person. Sugar was rationed to 200g (8oz) per person per month; there was also a monthly allowance of 400g (1lb) preserves. The average consumption of sugar is now over 3kg (6lb) per month, and a recent survey in Britain of 15,000 children being monitored in a Child Health and Education study group showed that 43 per cent of these 10-year-olds had sweets or chocolate every single day. Half of them had a sweet fizzy drink every day too. In addition, they also ate sugar-loaded cakes, biscuits, puddings and an enormous range of convenience foods, both sweet and savoury. Although sugar consumption in Britain appears to have gone down to 38kg (76lb) per head per year from its 1974 peak of 54kg (108lb) far too much sugar is eaten, still, in the form of ready-prepared foods.

Relieved as everyone was to leave war-time restrictions behind them, the truth of the matter is that never before had the British been healthier. Nor have they since. In the forty years that have elapsed since the war, the intake of fat and sugar has increased substantially, while consumption of 'complex carbohydrates', that is, the starchy foods like potatoes and grains and those with a high fibre content, have gone down. This reflects the common trend of dietary habits throughout the developed world.

Wholefoods

Wherever you can select uncomplicated 'whole' foods instead of the highly processed products of modern food technology, your health can only benefit. Wholefoods are complete foods with nothing added and nothing taken away. Grown or produced by natural means, they reach the consumer in or very close to their original state. They are foods which have not been refined, and to which no synthetic or inorganic chemicals, colouring or preservatives have been added.

Of course, some 'whole' foods do not quite live up to this definition if judged by the strictest criteria: whole flours produced simply by the milling process have an altered state (none the less, nothing has been added or taken away) and some dairy foods contain additives: for example, salt is added in the cheese-making process, but despite this farmhouse cheese is still regarded as a wholefood.

For the purposes of this book foods that do not fall into the wholefood category are refined white flours, sugars, grains, pasta and rice, and foods that have been processed in some way so that their original state has been altered; also excluded are those which include additional sugar, salt or other preservatives (such as, for example, canned vegetables).

Even commercially frozen vegetables are not exempt from additives. Although freezing *per se* does not interfere with the food's wholeness, salt – and even sugar – is added to many frozen foods. More complex made-up dishes may contain a range of additives. The ideal frozen foods are those which are home-frozen while extremely fresh, especially those which have been organically grown.

It is worth looking out for the canned vegetables which do not contain added salt; their availability is increasing. Canned fish, too, such as mackerel and tuna, are useful standbys, and though salt is usually added these are such good news in every other nutritional respect that they need not be excluded.

The key to a balanced diet

The best diet for health is a balanced one, each nutrient balancing another. What this means in practice is moderation in all foods, and perhaps a few changes of emphasis in both the proportions and the types of food eaten.

Food can be divided into nutritional categories – proteins, carbohydrates and sugars, fibre and fats – which, taken in balanced proportions, constitute a healthy diet. Protein is the substance that repairs and regenerates cells. It is also responsible for the formation of hormones, sexual development and rate of metabolism.

In the diet, protein breaks down into amino acids. Different types of protein contain different amino acids, and the body requires twenty-two made up in a specific pattern to manufacture human protein. All but eight of these can be made by the body. These eight 'essential' amino acids must be provided by the diet; they carry out their function of re-building body cells after absorption by the intestines.

If any of the eight essential amino acids fail to be supplied by the diet, no proper protein synthesis can be made within the body.

Meat and dairy foods contain all eight essential amino acids, but not all sources of protein do. Such foods are described as 'incomplete proteins'. Vegetarians need to pay special attention to balancing these incomplete proteins, and one way of doing this is to complement bean dishes with grain dishes so that the amino acids missing in one dish are made up in the other. This ensures that all the essential amino acids are consumed at one meal, thus enabling protein synthesis to take place.

Protein deficiency, a highly unusual condition in the Western world, can lead to the malformation of nails, skin and hair. Growth can also be affected, and mental retardation may result. The first symptoms of protein deficiency are lack of energy and stamina and slow recovery from illness, including slow healing of wounds. Body-building diets tend to be high in protein, but on the other hand there are some very successful vegetarian athletes who rely on 'carb loading' rather than protein supplements to ensure healthy cell regeneration.

Gluten, the protein contained in wheat and some other cereals (it is the component that makes dough stretchy) can be a problem for some people. Sufferers from coeliac disease are generally advised to avoid gluten, which causes malabsorption of nutrients. Those on gluten-free diets can obtain gluten-free flours and adapt to making bread and pastry from soya flour and otherwise using grains other than wheat – such as millet, for example.

Carbohydrates are chemical substances made up of carbon, hydrogen and oxygen. They provide energy, help to regulate the metabolism and enable fat to be broken down within the liver. Sugars, including those found in fresh fruit, are 'simple' carbohydrates. They are quickly absorbed and converted to glucose, or blood sugar, which fuels the brain, nervous system and muscles. Refined carbohydrates, such as white flour products, are broken down and assimilated too quickly to give sustained energy. 'Complex' carbohydrates come from foods such as whole grains, unrefined cereals and root vegetables. They are digested at a gradual rate and supply sustained energy as glucose is fed into the bloodstream at a steady rate. An important element in any healthy diet, complex carbohydrates are high in fibre – the 'woody' part of leaves, stems, roots, nuts, seeds and fruit which is not dealt with by the digestive enzymes in the gut. Fibre used to be called roughage, or sometimes 'unavailable carbohydrate', and that is exactly what it is – unavailable for use as a nutrient by the body.

Starches are another important group of carbohydrates. Cellulose is the most abundant, commonly found in vegetables and fruit but contributing little nourishment. However, it combines with other undigested polysaccarides to form the dietary fibre necessary for the efficient working of the bowels.

Many people suffer from a deficiency of dietary fibre, which can lead to various health problems, especially diverticular diseases but also heart disease, arthritis and cancer.

Carbohydrate deficiency is not a common problem, but many of us eat too much of the wrong sort. For example, most people consume far too much sugar, a contributory factor in a number of increasingly common diseases.

A high proportion of the body's energy requirement comes from fat, which carries more than twice the number of calories per gram than carbohydrate does. In addition to providing energy, fats are vehicles for the fat-soluble vitamins – A, D, E and K. A limited amount of fat in the diet is necessary, for it provides protection for such organs as the liver, kidneys and heart; however, too much of certain fats can damage these organs.

The diet of the Japanese is based on extremely fresh vegetables and fish. They have a low fat intake, and the incidence of heart disease in Japan is about one-quarter of that in England and Wales. This tells us something about the relationship between fat consumption and heart disease, both of which are far higher in the West. It could be argued that the Japanese are less genetically disposed to heart disease. However, when Japanese people move to the West and adopt a Western-style diet, they soon become as prone to heart disease as the indigenous population.

Fats are either saturated, mono-unsaturated or polyunsaturated. Saturated fat derives from animals and sets hard at room temperature. Apart from meat itself, the most common sources are dairy products such as cream and butter. Polyunsaturates derive from vegetable oils and are naturally liquid at room temperature, as are mono-unsaturates. Polyunsaturates are found naturally occurring in nuts and seeds. Mono-unsaturated fats cannot, like polyunsaturates, help to lower blood cholesterol levels, but neither do they raise it, like saturated fats. Olive oil is one example of a mono-unsaturated fat, containing between 4 and 14 per cent polyunsaturates depending on the crop and extraction.

Eating too much fat is universally condemned by the medical profession because it has been shown to contribute to obesity and, because it causes cholesterol build-up, to certain degenerative diseases, especially heart disease. Apart from cutting down on fats generally it is advisable to replace the saturated fats with polyunsaturates, such as sunflower oil. These not only do less harm than saturated fats but contribute in a beneficial way to health by improving metabolism of the saturated fats in the body and substantially lowering cholesterol levels in the blood.

In their eagerness to put this knowledge into practice, many people have reconciled themselves to giving up butter entirely in favour of polyunsaturated spreads. However, many of those who endorsed the new spreads wholeheartedly have recently been concerned to discover that polyunsaturated fats are not so beneficial that more is better. The aim should be to cut fat intake overall, not merely to replace one type with another. Butter is in any case an important source of nutrients, and tastes good. Use it, by all means, but with restraint.

One further complication in the fats/cholesterol controversy has arisen recently. A doctor has claimed that polyunsaturated fats lower cholesterol levels in the blood by driving it into the blood vessels. This could mean that hardening of the arteries is more likely to occur with these fats than with saturated animal fat. Perhaps in the end we might be better off with naturally produced butter than with any of the processed yellow fats.

In the average diet, about one-third of all the fat eaten comes from butter, margarine, lard and other fats and oils; another quarter comes from all kinds of meat; milk, cream and cheese provide about a fifth, and the rest comes from cakes, pastries, biscuits, eggs and other foods. Eating less of all these, removing obvious fat from meat, avoiding fried foods, using low-fat spreads instead of butter and ordinary margarine, yoghurt instead of full-fat cream, substituting curd cheese for full-fat cheese and replacing full-cream milk with skimmed milk are some of the easy ways to cut down fat consumption. Many other ideas will be found in the recipes later in the book.

Fried food is particularly unhealthy: if the body has to consume too much on a regular basis, the lymphatic system will react to produce symptoms of fatigue, headaches, viruses, colds, chills, backache and swollen glands.

Vitamins: the accessory factors

In 1881 research showed that animals could not be reared on proteins, fats, carbohydrates and mineral salts alone. Subsequently Gowland Hopkins established the presence of 'accessory factors' in milk. For these the name 'vitamines' was suggested, as they were considered to be amines, and amines are a constituent of protein. The term has survived for over a century, minus the 'e'. Present in many foodstuffs and essential for growth, vitamins cannot be manufactured by the body and must be ingested in food; deficiency will cause symptoms that can be eliminated only by the absent vitamin itself.

Vitamins are usually classified by their solubility. Fat-soluble vitamins, such as A, D, E and K, are not destroyed by cooking and can be stored in the body. Water-soluble vitamins, such as C and B-complex, can be destroyed by cooking and through manufacturing processes. They are not stored in the body and must be included in the diet daily.

Recent trends in food-preparation

Man's main sources of food have been, from the earliest times to the present century, animal flesh, fish, grains, seeds, nuts and fruit. Only in the last hundred years or so has the form in which these foods reached their consumers changed substantially, and over that period the incidence of a number of food-related diseases has increased considerably.

One of the results of the industrial revolution was that people began eating a larger and larger proportion of their meals away from home. A vast number of people now depend for part or all of their food intake on the mass catering facilities of factories, schools, hospitals, prisons and other institutions, and when food is prepared in bulk in a central kitchen and kept hot for one or two hours before being served many of its vitamins are lost.

Another of the principal changes that has occurred has been the rise of the food-processing industry, which has brought convenience, certainly, and largely eliminated the spread of disease by food contamination (milk, for example, was once a prominent disease-carrier). Modern food-preservation methods, such as freezing and canning, have undoubtedly extended the availability of many foods, particularly fruits and vegetables, and have therefore given all of us a more varied diet, and one less dependent on seasonal fluctuation. However, food-processing can often be detrimental to nutritional quality. Though lost nutrients can partly be compensated for by the addition of vitamins and minerals, such measures do not wholly restore the food's original nutritional value.

White flour is a good example. Until a century ago all flour was wholemeal – that is to say, the entire wheat grain was ground into flour. One of the drawbacks of this process was that the inclusion of wheatgerm in the flour severely limited its shelf-life. Three or four weeks after being ground, the wholemeal flour would develop unpleasant flavours. Also, certain of the nutrients were lost by this process. With the advent of roller milling in the late nineteenth century it became possible to separate out and remove the wheatgerm prior to milling the grain. In the course of this, the bran, or outer coating of the grain, was also removed. The end-product, however, which was chiefly derived from the starchy centre of the wheat grain, was a white flour which was stable in storage for many months. When it was realized that certain nutrients were lost in the roller-milling process legislation was introduced to ensure that some were put back: iron, calcium, vitamin B1 and niacin. None the less, substantial quantities of minerals such as phosphorus, magnesium, potassium, chromium, manganese, cobalt, copper, zinc and selenium are completely lost, together with the wheatgerm's vitamin E.

Writing in dismay about today's standard white loaf an American researcher claimed that of some twenty-five food elements known to be removed during processing only two or three were returned, and then only in a synthetic form. Frequently too much iodine was added, together

A dish of aubergines combined with tomatoes and seasoned with ginger, cumin, garlic and turmeric can make a substantial main course.

with the wrong kind of iron – one that is hard to assimilate. Usually no copper was added, and iron cannot be utilized without it. He also found several suspect chemicals.

Today's wholemeal flour, because it contains wheatgerm and wheatgerm contains oil which can affect its keeping qualities, is best not stored in quantity.

Refined white sugar, similarly, has lost most of the chromium, zinc and manganese present in raw brown sugar. Considerable loss of vitamins occurs also in the dehydration of food, and in canning and freezing.

Vitamins and minerals are essential to a balanced diet, and must be supplied in a form that the body will accept; eating refined foods is likely to mean denying them to the body, to the general detriment of health. Take vitamin E, an excellent natural anti-thrombin (that is, it prevents blood clots forming) that is highly beneficial to the heart: modern milling methods remove wheatgerm, which contains not only vitamin E but wheat oil, natural phosphates and active enzymes. To put vitamin E back into the diet, it is necessary to eat wholewheat grains, in wholewheat bread; other rich sources of this vitamin are nuts, watercress, spinach and safflower oil.

It is important to eat something from each of the natural food groups every day to achieve the 'balance' advocated by nutritionists. The six categories of natural foods are whole grains, pulses, vegetables, fruits, fats and proteins. Each of these encompasses a wide range of food items, as the table on pages 20–21 shows.

Junk foods

Junk food is, broadly speaking, food that contains artificial preservatives or additives or that has been so highly processed as to have very few of its original nutrients.

The effects of junk food on health depend on the level of intake and whether junk food is incidental to an otherwise healthy diet or has actually replaced it. Exercise is also a factor: physically active people are in a better position than others to work off the accumulated effects of a junk-food diet.

The main dangers of junk food are that it is likely to overload the system with fat and leave it vulnerable to a range of medical problems because of the amount of harmful additives it causes the body to absorb. All forms of processed and refined foods, preservatives and food additives can be the main catalysts for a virus infection. One of the best steps to take if you

A dish of haricot beans, dressed with egg, oils, onions and coriander would be satisfying for lunch. Accompany with wholemeal bread for a better-balanced meal.

Wholefoods

Fruits

Apples
Apricots
Bananas
Berry fruits
Cherries
Dates
Dried fruits, all varieties,
    for their concentrated
    sweetness coupled with
    high fibre content
Grapefruit
Grapes
Guavas
Kumquats
Lemons
Limes
Lychees
Mangos
Melons
Nectarines
Oranges and related
    fruits
Peaches
Pears
Pineapples
Plums
Quinces

Proteins

Dairy foods:
    cheeses, especially
    low-fat (e.g. ricotta,
    Edam)
    eggs
    skimmed milk
    goat's milk
    ewe's milk
Fish:
    oily fish (e.g.
    mackerel, salmon,
    tuna)
    white fish (e.g.
    haddock, cod)
Legumes
Meat:
    beef
    game
    lamb
    pork
    poultry
Nuts
Seeds
Whole grains

Fats

Avocados
Butter
Fish oils, including
    cod liver oil
Nut butters
Nut oils (e.g. coconut,
    peanut, walnut)
Olive oil
Olives
Polyunsaturated
    margarines and
    spreads
Safflower oil
Sesame, sunflower
    and other seed oils
Soya oil
Tahini
Wheatgerm oil

Wholefoods

Grains

Barley
Buckwheat
Corn
Millet
Oats
Rice
Rye
Wheat and its
    derivatives

Pulses

Aduki or adzuki beans
Black-eye beans
Broad beans
Chick peas
Foul beans
Kidney beans, all
    varieties
Lentils, all varieties
Mung beans
Split peas

Vegetables

Artichokes
Asparagus
Aubergines
Beans
Beetroot
Broccoli
Brussels sprouts
Cabbages
Carrots
Cauliflower

Celery	Leeks	Parsnips	Spinach
Corn	Lettuce	Peas	Sprouted grains
Courgettes	Mushrooms	Peppers	Swedes
Cucumber	Okra	Potatoes	Tomatoes
Garlic	Onions	Radishes	Turnips
Kohl rabi	Parsley	Sea kale	Watercress

feel a cold coming on is to cut fat intake and exist on plenty of fresh fruit and a few vegetables for a couple of days, to allow the system to eliminate accumulated toxins.

One recent report claims that 98 per cent of the important nutrients in many foods have been destroyed by one factor or another by the time meals reach the table. This '2 per cent' food can represent as much as 50 per cent of the average diet.

Even fresh foods sold commercially are not as fresh as they may appear. Oranges taken from the greengrocer's or supermarket shelf and randomly measured for vitamin C content showed as much as a 40 per cent difference in the individual levels. This does not mean that none of the oranges you buy will contain vitamin C, but it means that 'fresh' fruit and vegetables may not be supplying the levels of vitamins you think they are. The only answer to the problem is to be very careful with meal-planning.

American scientists have recently shown statistically that many man-made foods lack the essential trace elements found in natural foods. The original source of much synthetic food is petroleum, and it has been known to researchers for over three decades that petroleum causes cancer. Commercially produced confectionery, soft drinks and pastries have been shown to cause fluctuations in the blood sugar level that have affected the cortex – the part of the brain that governs perceptual functions. Benzoic acid, used in a wide array of products, has been found to impede growth and high doses can cause neurological disorders. Calcium disodium EDTA, widely used in 'fast' foods and canned drinks, has been known to cause liver lesions in young rats and kidney damage in humans. Processed vegetable oil extracts, used particularly in carbonated soft drinks, have been implicated in heart, liver, thyroid, testicle and liver damage.

The dangers of a junk-food diet speak for themselves.

Never before has food been so complicated – a reflection of our complex society. But above all never forget that you have a choice. If you do not want a healthy diet, no one will try to impose one on you. If you do, it is your choice and you must put some effort into attaining it. The chances are that by so doing you will derive greater pleasure from food than you ever did previously, and you will certainly be doing your health a favour.

CHAPTER ONE

Dairy foods and fats

Dairy foods, principally in the form of milk, butter and cheese, are one of the main sources of fat in the Western diet – and fat, especially the saturated kind, is a substance of which most of us consume too much. For those of us who grew up on school milk, bread and butter and positive encouragement to eat cheese, the fact that these natural products of an ancient farming tradition are not altogether desirable foods may come as something of a shock.

The problem with the high levels of saturated fats contained in these dairy foods is that they are widely believed to increase the amount of cholesterol, a fatty substance thought to contribute to heart disease, in the bloodstream.

Fat intake can be drastically reduced by substituting low-fat skimmed milk for full-fat milk, polyunsaturated fats for butter, yoghurt for cream and low-fat cheeses for high-fat cheeses. The recipes in this chapter show how these ingredients can be substituted for more traditional ingredients. (It is also helpful to cut down on fried foods.)

First, however, it is necessary to be able to distinguish between the different forms of fat. Fats are built up from smaller units known as fatty acids which, in turn, are made up of atoms of carbon, hydrogen and oxygen. Saturated fatty acids have all the hydrogen their molecule can accommodate. Unsaturated fatty acids are short of two or more hydrogen atoms in each molecule of fatty acid, while polyunsaturated fatty acid molecules are short of at least four hydrogen atoms. All the fats we eat comprise a wide variety of different fatty acids, some of which will be saturated, some unsaturated and some polyunsaturated.

Usually fats derived from animals have a higher proportion of saturated fatty acids than those from plants. There are exceptions to this general rule. For example, the oils in fish, an animal food, are mainly unsaturated, whereas coconut oil has far more saturated fatty acids than other vegetable oils. (Chicken, turkey, offal and rabbit have lower fat contents than red carcass meat.)

Generally speaking, the harder a fat is at room temperature the more saturated fatty acids it contains. Compare, for example, the consistency of butter, which contains roughly 50 per cent saturated fatty acids, with that of a soft margarine, which may contain only 18 per cent saturated fatty acids.

Butter has recently gained a rather bad reputation, owing to its saturated fat content. Many purists have banished it from their diets altogether, but it is not necessary to give up the taste of butter in order to achieve a healthy diet – besides which, it contains valuable nutrients and is, generally speaking, a natural food. Rather than outlawing butter try, instead, to think of it in a new way. Instead of automatically using it to spread on bread, consider healthier alternatives such as a low-fat polyunsaturated spread, or tahini, or an avocado or nut spread: cutting your butter intake in this respect means you can use it in another dish where its taste will not be masked by other substances.

However, there is butter and butter. Commercially produced 'salted' butter can contain inorganic sodium chloride, sodium carbonate or calcium carbonate, colouring and preservative. Aim to buy butter that has been as naturally produced as possible, so that its full range of nutrients are intact and it contains no potentially harmful additives.

Milk, too, in its most popular form, contains a high proportion of saturated fat. Whole milk consists of fat globules connected by whey. The thought of changing to anything other than the full-fat milk to which you are accustomed may be alarming at first, but consider the advantages of changing to low-fat skimmed milk: it keeps better, because it contains less fat to go rancid and produce off flavours and smells, and it is less likely to cause cholesterol build-up. Ideally, you should aim to cut your total milk intake. Why not try switching from white coffee to black, and from Indian tea, which contains high levels of undesirable tannin, to Chinese tea or one of the herbal teas that do not need milk?

On breakfast cereals, such as muesli, natural low-fat yoghurt can be used instead of milk; pure fruit juice is another possibility – orange, pineapple or almost any flavour is suitable. Fruit juice can also be used in baking to make up the liquid quantity where milk has been reduced. For sauces, try a combination of yoghurt and skimmed milk, or yoghurt on its own.

For example, the 'new' way of making a roux, or white sauce, is to combine wholemeal flour with fat then mix in a little skimmed milk to form a smooth consistency. Then add in the required amount of yoghurt and cook over a gentle heat until the mixture has thickened.

Milk is a good protein source; also, as well as vitamins A, D, and E and some of the B-complex ones, it contains the minerals calcium and phosphorus. However, some people are allergic to milk. The enzyme lactase is required so that the lactose, or milk sugar, which is present in cow's milk can be digested. Those who lack this enzyme will develop an allergic reaction.

Cow's milk also contains thyroxine, a hormone which controls the glandular system, metabolism, the nervous system, mental development and growth rate. Cow's milk is designed essentially for calves, who have a growth rate four times that of humans. Excessive consumption of cow's milk may lead in some cases to physical and possibly mental imbalances. Its nutrients, on the other hand, can be supplied by other foods, particularly vegetables. Broccoli, kale, spinach and parsley, for example, are all extremely good sources of calcium – and of vitamin A. Vitamin D, on the other hand, is found in fish: salmon, sardine and tuna, for example, and fish liver oils such as cod and halibut. It is also found in sunshine.

Some people have a tendency to form mucus, and for them milk, together with butter, cheese and cream, is potentially harmful because it can contribute to excessive mucus build-up, leading to conditions such as sinusitis, nasal congestion and excess sputum. Yoghurt can actually help to eliminate mucus, as can fruit, vegetables and nuts. Oranges, for instance, are an excellent alternative to milk, containing many of the same nutrients (including calcium and vitamin A). Peaches and oranges both have the ability to help disperse mucus.

Low-fat yoghurt is an excellent food. It contains about 5 per cent high-grade protein and only about 10 per cent fat. A pint of it (600 ml) contains less than 250 calories, and it can be used instead of cream in almost any recipe. Making it at home is easy, and works out cheaper than the cheaper brands on the market. Its nutritional advantages stem from the fact that it is a predigested dairy product, so the body finds it easier to digest than milk, butter or cheese. As the skimmed milk from which yoghurt is made changes into yoghurt, it gains more nutrients and thus becomes a more valuable food than the skimmed milk.

Yoghurt has been implicated in aiding recovery from all sorts of modern diseases and in promoting longevity. Many ethnic recipes make liberal use of yoghurt, especially those from the Middle and Far East.

For the purposes of this book, yoghurt means naturally produced, additive-free low-fat yoghurt. When using it in recipes, the only special characteristic to note is that it should not be boiled hard. Otherwise, it is easy to produce a smooth thickened sauce from yoghurt. It can be stabilized by adding a little cornflour and stirring in well; alternatively, whisk in an egg white.

Of the various types of cream commonly available, the highest in fat content is double cream (minimum 48 per cent), followed by whipping cream (minimum 35 per cent), single cream and soured cream (minimum 18 per cent).

'Real dairy ice cream' and other commercially produced ice creams are among the worst of all manufactured foods in terms of nutrition: 'real dairy ice cream' is laden with saturated fat and sugar, while other types are likely to have been made with vegetable fats together with a list of additives that would seem to be more appropriate to the garden shed than the freezer (see Chapter 3). Do not let the word 'dairy' deceive you. All in all, you would do much better to make your own ice cream. Then, if you do use cream, you can at least control the quantity. And you can base your ice cream on yoghurt, for a highly nutritious, low-fat sweet.

A true dairy food, and an indispensable one, is cheese. Cheese is the best source, apart from sesame seeds, of calcium available, and is also high in vitamin A. However, it does present certain problems: it has a high salt content and contains a large proportion of saturated fat. Some types also contain colouring and preservatives.

The cheeses to avoid are the processed ones: try instead to obtain traditional or modern natural cheeses, and choose the new low-fat versions whenever possible, or low-fat cheese made from yoghurt. Many of the recipes in this book call for low-fat Cheddar, which has a 15 per cent fat content as compared with 30–37 per cent fat in the regular Cheddars (and, indeed, most hard cheeses). Dutch Edam, made from skimmed milk, also has a lower calorie count than, for example, regular Cheddar. Continental cheeses, such as Brie and mozzarella, are a little lower in fat than traditional English ones. Lowest of all is the doubly skimmed ricotta, which is useful for pasta sauces.

It can be useful to combine cheese with dishes that contain a high proportion of vegetables or fruit to ensure a good nutritional balance. Eating fruit and vegetables with cheese, too, will have a cleansing effect and provide some protection from the cheese's tendency to stimulate mucus production.

There is one type of cheese which brings together many of the advantages we look for in food: low-fat, low-calorie and infinitely versatile, cottage cheese has rightly gained a large following since it was first produced commercially in the 1950s.

In medieval times when most families' dairy needs were supplied by their own cow, pans of fresh milk would be left every day for the cream to rise to the top, later to be skimmed off for making butter, and the skimmed milk to set, forming curds and whey. The whey was drained from the curd, through muslin, and became cottage cheese. Cottage cheese is still made like this, but a specially prepared culture is added to the separated milk to produce a curd. The curd is cut, the whey drained off, and the curd is then washed with chilled, purified water; finally it is mixed with salt and cultured cream to produce the mild-flavoured and distinctively textured cheese we know today.

As cottage cheese contains protein, calcium and B vitamins it is a useful part of a regular balanced diet and can either be eaten on its own or with other foods. Per 100 g (approximately 4 oz) it contains 12 g protein, 3 g fat and 3 g carbohydrate, and there is now additionally a kind which has only 1.5 g fat per 100 g. It is well-known, too, as an ideal food for slimmers on a calorie-controlled diet, containing only 100 calories, approximately, per 100 g. Snack lunches are another of its roles, for cottage cheese can provide a fresh, nutritious, well-balanced, low-calorie mini-meal just on its own. Its mild flavour combines well with a wide variety of sweet and savoury foods. It goes well with cress and lettuce, on or with crispbread or wholemeal bread; it can be used to stuff a baked potato or omelette – added quickly towards the end of the cooking so that it does not 'run away', and can be added to dips, pâtés, sauces, stuffings, soups, flans, desserts, cakes and tarts. It also makes a delicious cheese topping on toast, pasta and vegetables, heated under the grill.

Another food that springs to mind when we think of dairy products is eggs. Recent evidence seems to have exonerated them from the criticisms of a few years ago when it was thought that because a large egg contains about 250 mg of cholesterol it could therefore be supposed to increase the level of cholesterol in the blood. The findings of the University of California have been that there is 'no satisfactory statistically-significant correlation between the number of eggs we consume and the level of cholesterol in our blood'.

The reasons for this are because the waxy substance lecithin, found in egg yolk, acts as an effective emulsifying agent which dissolves cholesterol before it reaches the linings of the artery wall. As a large egg contains about ten times as much lecithin as it does cholesterol eggs may well serve to lower blood cholesterol and thus reduce the risk of heart disease.

Other benefits have been discovered too: the lecithin from two average eggs (containing about 5 g) eaten daily over a three-week period will increase the choline content of the brain by about 500 per cent. Choline is part of the vitamin B-complex and is essential for efficient brain functioning. As a result of this research, carried out by the Massachusetts Institute of Technology, lecithin is now being used by doctors in the treatment of short-term loss of memory.

Eggs are also an excellent source of protein. Over 90 per cent of the protein content of eggs is usable. This protein comprises all eight essential amino acids, needed by the body for cell growth and repair. These amino acids are the ones which must be provided from the diet because the body cannot produce its own.

Finally, eggs are a very rich source of vitamins – A, B1, B2, B3 and E – and the minerals phosphorus, potassium, iron, sodium, zinc, magnesium, sulphur, selenium and calcium.

Raw eggs should be regarded with caution, because they contain avidin, a glycoprotein which if eaten raw destroys biotin in the diet. Biotin is part of the B-complex group of vitamins, essential for the metabolism of fat and protein. Cooking the eggs destroys the avidin. Unless you are in the habit of eating prairie oysters, keeping off raw eggs should not be a problem.

What of the arguments over battery and free-range eggs? In nutrition terms, the answer is not so straightforward. Free-range eggs contain 50 per cent more folic acid, a member of the B-complex group of vitamins essential in guarding against anaemia, than battery eggs and also more vitamin B12, but battery eggs can contain more iron. On the debit side, battery eggs contain more sodium.

Perhaps more important than that argument is the question of cholesterol in egg dishes generally. The traditional way to serve eggs is in a creamy (high in cholesterol) sauce. However, by retaining the eggs and re-thinking the sauce you can produce old favourites with a new and healthy slant.

Non-dairy fats

Though marketed as a natural companion to butter, there is nothing natural about margarine, nor anything wholesome or health-giving (the low-fat, polyunsaturated spreads are here excluded). Its ingredients are oil, often unspecified, emulsifying salts, preservatives, flavouring, colouring and a host of other additives. Most varieties contain as much saturated fat as butter and just as many calories, but lack any of butter's redeeming features. Even the so-called nutrients in margarine are added in artificially after processing. Some scientists do not consider margarine suitable for human consumption.

When margarine was first developed, by a French scientist in 1860, it was made from beef tallow. As technology advanced vegetable oils were used in its manufacture, as they are today. This should mean that margarine contains more unsaturated oils than butter. However, in the process of converting the liquid oils into a solid yellow fat, hydrogenation (the passing of hydrogen through the fats) takes place, changing many of the polyunsaturates into trans-fatty acids. While polyunsaturates improve fat metabolism and help to keep down cholesterol levels in the blood, these trans-fatty acids do not act in the same way and may even be more hazardous than saturated fats.

Many vegetable cooking fats, margarines and a vast range of baking goods and processed foods are made from oil products high in trans-fatty acids. Lard, for example, is a vegetable fat sold in block form, solid at room temperature and highly saturated. It has no place in any healthy diet.

For a basic substance to spread on bread, the best of all possible worlds is to make your own spread by combining additive-free, naturally produced dairy butter with an equal quantity of cold pressed oil – for example, safflower, sunflower or sesame oil. (Rape seed oil is another possibility that has recently performed well in tests.) The result is a creamy, spreadable fat with a good taste, high in polyunsaturates, salt-free and free of other additives.

Choose your oil as carefully as you would wine. Read the label carefully, buy something from a stated, polyunsaturated source (sunflower, safflower, corn, soya or sesame, for example) and look for the words 'cold pressed', otherwise you will be buying something which has lost the benefits of being polyunsaturated through processing. The oil you buy should be a good colour, throw a sediment and actually smell of the ingredient from which it is made. Cold pressed sesame oil is a thick, dark brown with a sediment and a heavy, pungent smell. However, the most commonly available cooking oils, including those labelled simply 'vegetable oil', have been extracted from their source by means of chemical solvents and heat processes. In order to make them clean-tasting, colourless and clear, further processing, preservation and bleaching techniques are employed. While these combined techniques certainly serve to extract every last drop of oil, they leave an unacceptable level of chemical residue. It is worth noting, perhaps, that the solvents used in oil processing are comparable with those used in the dry-cleaning industry.

In their natural state most oils have a built-in preservative to prevent them from becoming rancid too quickly. This natural preservative is vitamin E, of which the richest sources are wheatgerm and safflower oil. During processing most of the vitamin E content is lost, which is why artificial preservatives have to be added.

The pure oils *are* more expensive, but the extra expense is wholly justifiable in this case.

Home-made yoghurt

Yoghurt is the all-purpose cream substitute. It can be used in any recipe that calls for cream, though it is never likely to be acceptable in coffee.

*2 tablespoons (30 ml) low-fat
natural live yoghurt*

*3 tablespoons (45 ml) dried
skimmed milk powder*
1 pint (600 ml) low-fat milk

Mix together the yoghurt and milk powder to form a smooth paste. Warm the milk to 105–110°F (40–45°C), or until you can just bear to hold your fingers in it. Beat the yoghurt mixture and milk together and pour into a wide-necked vacuum flask. Leave overnight.

If you have a gas oven the yoghurt mixture can be turned into a ceramic bowl and left in the oven, with just the pilot light on, overnight to 'set'.

If you have an electric yoghurt-maker, the procedure is foolproof. After mixing together the yoghurt and milk powder just follow the manufacturers' instructions.

Refrigerate the yoghurt before use.

Yoghurt sauce

This smooth, tasty sauce based on cooked yoghurt is an ideal accompaniment for Indian or other highly seasoned food.

whole spices

powdered cumin, coriander and other spices

Dry-fry the whole spices, then add in the powdered ones until the spices give off a good, pungent smell. Remove from the heat and stir in as much yoghurt as is required. Return to a lower heat and continue cooking.

Eggs in creamy sauce

SERVES 2 AS A SUPPER DISH

4 eggs, hard-boiled
1 tablespoon (15 ml) wholemeal flour
2 teaspoons (10 ml) mustard powder

½ pint (300 ml) natural low-fat yoghurt
freshly ground black pepper

Shell the eggs and slice in half. Arrange in an ovenproof dish. Whisk together the flour, mustard and yoghurt, using a liquidizer or hand whisk. Season. Turn the yoghurt mixture into a non-stick saucepan and gently bring it to the boil, stirring all the time. When thickened, pour over the eggs. Brown under the grill before serving.

New cheese sauce

This goes particularly well with hot steamed vegetables.

oil
1 small onion, finely chopped, or a piece of leek, or the equivalent quantity of chives, chopped well
1 tomato, chopped to a pulp

2 oz (50 g) low-fat hard cheese, grated
2 oz (50 g) curd cheese
4 tablespoons (60 ml) low-fat milk
1 egg
freshly ground black pepper

Oil a non-stick saucepan. Add the onion and tomato and cook until a sauce-like consistency results. Add the cheeses, milk and egg. Stir over a gentle heat until thickened. Season with pepper.

Egg cheese soufflé

SERVES 2

1 oz (25 g) polyunsaturated
margarine
1 oz (25 g) wholemeal flour
1 tablespoon (15 ml) mustard
powder

½ pint (300 ml) skimmed milk
3 eggs, separated
4 oz (100 g) half-fat Cheddar or gruyère
cheese, grated
pinch cayenne

Make a basic sauce with the fat, flour, mustard and milk. Simmer over a low heat until completely cooked and smooth. (If the sauce either curdles or separates remove it from the heat and place in a liquidizer goblet. Liquidize until smooth, then return to the pan.) Remove from the heat. Whisk the egg yolks until pale. Add a little at a time to the sauce. Stir well. Add the cheese and cayenne. Stiffly whisk the egg whites and carefully fold them into the mixture. Pour into a large, oiled soufflé dish and bake at 350°F/180°C/Gas 4 for 45 minutes until well risen and golden. Sprinkle with summer savory leaves and serve immediately.

To vary, add gently sautéed onions and/or steamed asparagus with the cheese.

Ultimate cheese scones

8 oz (255 g) wholemeal flour
½ teaspoon (2.5 ml) bicarbonate of
soda
½ teaspoon (2.5 ml) cream of tartar
½ teaspoon (2.5 ml) mustard powder
pinch cayenne

1½ oz (40 g) polyunsaturated margarine
4 oz (100 g) low-fat mature Cheddar,
grated
3 tablespoons (45 ml) skimmed milk
¼ pint (150 ml) natural low-fat yoghurt

Combine the first five ingredients and mix well. Add the margarine and mix until it resembles fine breadcrumbs. Add three-quarters of the cheese and mix well with the milk and yoghurt. Turn out on to a floured surface, knead lightly and roll out to ½-inch (1-cm) thickness. Cut rounds using a plain cutter. Sprinkle the remaining cheese over the scones. Place on an oiled baking tray and bake at 400°F/200°C/Gas 6 for 15–20 minutes until well risen and golden brown.

These are too delicious not to eat straight away. They make excellent lunch rolls split and filled with curd cheese and alfalfa sprouts, chopped egg and cress or fish fillets (possibly prawns) and salad.

Grainy cottage cheese slice

This makes an unusual side dish for dinner parties instead of a savoury
bread. It would go well with a fish main course
to make the meal more substantial.

*1 pint (600 ml) salt-free vegetable
  stock*
4 oz (100 g) toasted buckwheat
*8 oz (225 g) plain low-fat cottage
  cheese*
2 large eggs
*1 tablespoon (15 ml) chopped
  parsley*

*4 spring onions or small bunch chives,
  chopped*
1 teaspoon (5 ml) chopped basil
pinch savory
freshly ground black pepper
½ teaspoon (2.5 ml) sweet paprika

Bring the stock to the boil. Add the buckwheat and cook for 40 minutes or
until all liquid has been absorbed. The buckwheat should have more than
trebled in volume.

Sieve or liquidize the cottage cheese. Add to the buckwheat in a bowl
and mix well. Separate the eggs. Beat the yolks until pale and add them
into the cheese. Add the herbs. Beat the egg whites until stiff, and add into
the mixture gently. Season with black pepper and paprika. Pour into an
oiled shallow oblong tin, preferably non-stick, and smooth the surface.

Bake at 400°F/200°C/Gas 6 for 30 minutes until the top is browned and
the centre firm.

Cheese pâté

Served as a starter, this new version is much lower in
fat than traditional recipes.

SERVES 4

1 small onion, finely chopped
1 garlic clove, crushed
*4 oz (100 g) low-fat hard cheese (e.g.
  low-fat Cheshire)*
4 oz (100 g) cottage cheese

1 tablespoon (15 ml) low-fat yoghurt
1 tablespoon (15 ml) mustard powder
1 teaspoon (5 ml) prepared grain mustard
2 tablespoons (30 ml) chopped walnuts
2 small pickled cucumbers

This dish is quickly and easily prepared in a food processor. By hand each
stage will take a little longer.

Process or mince the onion and garlic. Add the hard cheese, then the
cottage cheese, yoghurt and mustards. Mix in the walnuts. Add one
cucumber. Spoon into a small soufflé dish, earthenware pot or individual
ramekins. Garnish with the remaining cucumber, cut into long, thin
slithers. Chill well before serving.

Pasta wheat salad

4 oz (100g) wholemeal cut macaroni
2 oz (50g) wheat berries, soaked
8 oz (225g) french beans, cut into
   small pieces
2 carrots, diced
4 spring onions, chopped
1 tablespoon (15ml) lovage
½ teaspoon (2.5ml) dill weed
½ teaspoon (2.5ml) basil

freshly ground pepper
DRESSING:
   4 oz (100g) ricotta cheese (or other
     low-fat, slightly crumbly curd
     cheese)
   2 teaspoons (10ml) prepared grain
     mustard
   lemon juice to taste

Cook the macaroni in plenty of boiling water until *al dente*. Drain. Boil the wheat berries in plenty of boiling water for about 30 minutes until well cooked; drain. Steam the beans until cooked but still crunchy. Combine the still-warm pasta, berries, beans, carrots, onions and herbs. Season with pepper.

For the dressing, liquidize (or whisk) the cheese, mustard and lemon juice. Add this dressing to the salad and toss well. Adjust the seasoning and serve. (Make the dressing and add to the cooked ingredients while they are still warm so that they absorb the flavours effectively.)

Savoury corn cake

This can either complement a main course or be served as main course
accompanied by a green leaf vegetable.

SERVES 4

4 oz (100g) corn meal
1 oz (25g) butter
4 oz (100g) low-fat cheese, grated

2 small home-made sausages, cooked
   (see page 81)
freshly ground black pepper

In a non-stick pan dry-fry the corn meal gently until it turns a pale beige colour. Put 7 fl oz (200ml) water in a saucepan. Pour in the hot corn meal – it should hiss. Simmer for about 5 minutes over a low heat until it thickens and begins to splutter. Reduce the heat to very low, cover the pan and allow to simmer for 20 minutes. Stir occasionally to prevent sticking.

Remove the lid and stir the mixture continuously until a spoon drawn through the mixture leaves wide tracks in the bottom of the pan (about 5 minutes). Season.

Remove from the heat and stir in the butter. Chop the sausage into very fine pieces. Stir 3 oz (75g) of the cheese and the chopped sausage into the mixture. Oil a 7-inch (18-cm) non-stick sandwich tin. Pour in the mixture and bake at 375°F/190°C/Gas 5 for 40 minutes. Remove and allow to cool.

Leave to set in the refrigerator for at least 1 hour. Serve the cake in wedges, sprinkle on the remaining cheese and heat through under the grill until the cheese is hot and bubbling.

Dill yoghurt dressing

This goes particularly well with eggs, fish and potatoes. Increase the quantity of dill if using the fresh herb.

*¼ pint (450ml) natural low-fat
    yoghurt
1 teaspoon (5ml) made mustard
2 tablespoons (30ml) lime juice
½ teaspoon (2.5ml) kelp powder
1 teaspoon (5ml) basil*

*2 teaspoons (10ml) dill weed
½ teaspoon (2.5ml) fennel seeds,
    crushed but not powdered
1 spring onion, minced
1 clove garlic, pressed
freshly ground black pepper*

Combine all the ingredients in a liquidizer and serve.

Stilton stuffed pears

SERVES 6 AS STARTER, 3 AS LIGHT LUNCHEON MAIN DISH

*8oz (225g) low-fat cottage cheese
    with onion and chives
¼ pint (150ml) milk
4oz (100g) Stilton cheese*

*2oz (50g) low-fat spread
3 ripe dessert pears
lettuce or watercress
chives or parsley*

Place the cottage cheese and milk in a liquidizer and blend until smooth and thick. Mash together the Stilton and low-fat spread to make a smooth purée. Peel the pears and cut them in half. Using a teaspoon, remove their cores. Use the Stilton mixture to fill the pear cavities. Set the pears on a bed of lettuce or watercress, spoon over the cottage cheese sauce and sprinkle with snipped chives or chopped parsley.

Cottage cheese fritters

MAKES 6–8

1½ oz (40g) wholemeal flour
6oz (175g) cottage cheese
1oz (25g) polyunsaturated margarine
3 eggs, separated

pinch cumin
freshly ground black pepper
a few snipped chives
a little oil

Mix the flour with the cottage cheese, margarine, egg yolks, seasoning and chives. Whisk the egg whites until stiff. Fold into the cheese mixture.

Oil a non-stick pan lightly and heat. Drop tablespoons of the mixture into the pan, spaced well apart. Fry over a moderate heat for 2–3 minutes until golden brown and cooked.

Azerbaidjan loaf

This dish makes an excellent centrepiece for large dinner parties.

2 tablespoons (30ml) dried yeast
1 teaspoon (5ml) soft brown sugar
9 fl oz (250ml) skimmed milk, warmed
14oz (400g) wholemeal flour
4oz (100g) polyunsaturated
    margarine

8oz (225g) low-fat Cheddar
2 eggs (one for glazing)
1 lb (450g) low-fat goat cheese
1 tablespoon (15ml) mustard
    powder
oil

Mix the yeast with the sugar and milk and leave in a warm place to become frothy. Then mix the flour with the yeast mixture in a large basin and add the margarine. Continue to beat until a dough is formed. Turn out on to a floured board and knead until elastic. Leave the dough to rise until doubled in size (about 2 hours). Knead again and return the dough to a warm place to rest. Grate the Cheddar cheese and beat in an egg, the goat cheese and the mustard until fully amalgamated.

Roll out the dough to a large round and place in a shallow, 10-inch (25-cm) oiled tin with the dough overlapping the sides. Pile the filling into the centre. Gather in the dough overlapping the tin, folding it as you go to form pleats. Gather the excess into the centre and twist into a neat knot-shape. Leave in a warm place for 20 minutes. Glaze with egg mixed with few drops of water. Bake at 375°F/190°C/Gas 5 for 1 hour until golden.

Turn out on to a wire rack and cool slightly before serving. Cut and serve at the dining-table.

A platter of raw vegetables can make an ideal first course on their own or served as crudités.

Neopolitan macaroni

Sunflower seeds are not traditional to this recipe but they do make a good wholefood addition, by increasing the nutrient content of the dish, and by imparting a nutty flavour to the topping.

SERVES 4

olive oil

1 small onion, chopped

1 clove garlic, crushed

1 small green pepper, diced,
    reserving some in strips

1 lb (450g) tomatoes, chopped

1 teaspoon (5ml) tomato purée

freshly ground black pepper

1 teaspoon (5ml) basil

2 teaspoons (10ml) oregano

8oz (225g) wholemeal macaroni

2 eggs, beaten

4 tablespoons (60ml) yoghurt

chilli seasoning

4oz (100g) low-fat Cheddar, grated
    (or mozzarella)

1 tablespoon (15ml) sunflower seeds

Heat a little olive oil in a frying-pan and sauté the onion and garlic. Add the pepper, reserving the strips for decoration. Add the tomatoes, purée, black pepper and herbs. Simmer for about 30 minutes until the consistency resembles that of a thick sauce. Meanwhile cook the macaroni in boiling water until just tender. Drain.

Combine the pasta with the beaten eggs and a sprinkling of oil and yoghurt. Add a pinch of chilli seasoning. Pour into a shallow oiled dish. Pour over the tomato sauce and herbs and top with the grated cheese. Sprinkle over the seeds. Arrange the retained strips of pepper in a criss-cross pattern on top and bake at 400°F/200°C/Gas 6 for 10 minutes, until bubbling and golden.

Egg consommé

SERVES 4

4 slices wholemeal bread

4 small eggs

2 pints (1 litre) good, strong consommé

a little grated hard cheese

Toast the bread. Put the toast into four ovenproof soup bowls. Break the eggs on to each piece of toast (so that the yolks remain whole). In a separate saucepan bring the consommé almost to the boil and allow to heat through. Ladle gently into soup bowls. Place in a low oven, 325°F/160°C/Gas 3, until the eggs have set. Sprinkle with cheese to serve.

Pulses combined with tomatoes and other natural ingredients can make a hearty stew for a cold winter's day.

Egg patties

These are good as a starter, or as part of a lunch.

SERVES 4

5 eggs (4 hard-boiled, 1 beaten)
1 slice home-boiled bacon (possibly leftovers)
1 tablespoon (15 ml) polyunsaturated margarine
1 onion, chopped
1 tablespoon (15 ml) chervil

1 tablespoon (15 ml) snipped chives
freshly ground black pepper
½ pint (300 ml) thick 'white' sauce
soft wholemeal breadcrumbs
oil
1 lemon

Chop the hard-boiled eggs. Finely chop the bacon. Sauté in the margarine with the onion, chervil, chives and pepper. Combine with the chopped egg and mix with the white sauce (see page 23). Form the mixture roughly into balls and chill.

When firm, shape each one into a ball then flatten the top and bottom slightly. Dip in the beaten egg and coat in breadcrumbs. Lightly oil a large non-stick frying-pan. Heat, then brown the patties on both sides.

Serve immediately, while very hot, with lemon wedges.

Poached egg curry

This curry makes a good luncheon dish for two or may be served as part of an Indian meal.

SERVES 2

1 large onion, sliced
2–3 large garlic cloves, pressed
1 piece root ginger, to taste, finely chopped
2 tablespoons (20 ml) oil
1 small stick cinnamon, broken up
1 teaspoon (5 ml) turmeric
1 teaspoon (5 ml) coriander

2 cardamoms, crushed
1 eating apple, cored but not peeled, minced
2 tomatoes, sliced
½ pint (300 ml) yoghurt
4 eggs
about 4 raw onions sliced
whole coriander leaves, separated

Sauté the onions, garlic and ginger in oil. Add the spices and 'fry'. Add the apple and tomatoes. Then gently add the yoghurt and 'fry', but do not allow to boil vigorously otherwise the yoghurt will separate. Simmer for 10 minutes.

Break the eggs gently, one at a time, into the curry sauce mix, keeping the whites together. Lower the heat, cover and cook for 20 minutes. Serve garnished with the separated onion rings and coriander leaves.

Spiced spinach and eggs

SERVES 2 AS MAIN COURSE, 4 AS SIDE DISH

2 lb (900 g) spinach
freshly ground black pepper
½ teaspoon (2.5 ml) ground cumin

½ teaspoon (2.5 ml) ground
  fenugreek
4 eggs

Wash and chop the spinach and ram into a saucepan with the spices. Cook until it is mushy and any liquid has evaporated. Place the spinach in a shallow ovenproof dish. Make four egg-sized indentations.

Break the eggs into each hole and bake at 350°F/180°C/Gas 4 for 15–20 minutes until the eggs are set. Serve with yoghurt.

Fluffy green omelette

This light and airy omelette takes only a few minutes to make and is well balanced in nutritional terms because the green elements contain vitamin C, the one vitamin eggs lack.

SERVES 2

4 medium eggs, separated
large bunch continental parsley
bunch watercress

1 onion, chopped very finely
freshly ground black pepper

Whisk the egg yolks until pale cream in colour. Whisk the whites until frothy. Finely chop the parsley and break the watercress into small sprigs. Fold the parsley and onion into the yolks and the egg whites into the yolks. Heat a non-stick omelette pan and pour in the mixture.

Agitate the surface of the egg mixture until most of the liquid has run through to the bottom and the top is cooked. Lay the watercress in a neat line down the centre of the omelette. Season. Fold in half and serve.

(If you wish to coagulate all the liquid egg, flash the omelette under a pre-heated grill for a few minutes until the top is quite cooked. Fold as before and serve.)

Egg baked potatoes

4 large potatoes

1 oz (25 g) butter or polyunsaturated
  spread

1 small onion, chopped

freshly ground black pepper

½ teaspoon (2.5 ml) nutmeg

2 tablespoons (30 ml) tomato
  purée

4 tablespoons (60 ml) curd cheese

4 tablespoons (60 ml) yoghurt

4 eggs

watercress

Wash, prick and bake the potatoes at 375°F/190°C/Gas 5 for 1½ hours. Allow the potatoes to become cool enough to handle. Slice lids off the potatoes and carefully scoop out the flesh into a bowl. Cream with the butter until smooth. Add the onion and seasoning. Beat in the tomato purée, cheese and yoghurt.

Replace the mixture in the skins and hollow out the tops. Carefully break the eggs into the hollows. Replace the potatoes in the oven for about 20 minutes until the eggs are set. To serve, garnish with watercress and top with potato lids.

Rice baked with curried eggs

8 oz (225 g) brown rice, cooked

1 tablespoon (15 ml) oil or clarified
  butter

1 small onion, minced

1 small eating apple, cored and
  minced

1 tablespoon (15 ml) wholemeal flour

¾ pint (450 ml) stock

2 teaspoons (10 ml) curry paste

4 eggs

2 tablespoons (30 ml) coriander
  leaves, chopped

Place the cooked rice in a large, deep baking dish. Make four wells, equally spaced, in the rice. Melt the oil or butter in a pan and add the onion and apple. Stir in the flour. Carefully add the stock and bring to the boil, stirring. Add the curry paste and when a smooth sauce has formed cook for a further few minutes. Spoon approximately a third of the sauce over the rice, ensuring it goes down into the wells. Break an egg into each well and spoon the rest of the sauce over the dish.

Place in a pre-heated oven, 375°F/190°C/Gas 5, and bake for about 25 minutes until the eggs are set. Sprinkle with coriander and serve.

Savoury souffléd bread pudding

This dish makes an ideal light lunch with a green salad.

SERVES 2

low-fat spread
2 slices soft wholemeal bread
4 oz (100 g) low-fat hard cheese
¾ pint (450 ml) low-fat milk

1 egg
freshly ground black pepper
nutmeg

'Butter' the bread thinly and place one piece on the bottom of a small, oiled, rectangular pie-dish. Sprinkle in the cheese and place the other slice of bread on top. Beat the egg well and whisk in the milk and seasonings. Pour over the bread and leave to soak in for 20–30 minutes or so. Bake at 450°F/230°C/Gas 8 for 20–30 minutes until well risen and golden. Serve immediately.

To vary, spread the bread with hummus or any home-made vegetable pâté. This produces an earthier flavour. Alternatively, halve the cheese quantity and use a good sprinkling of sprouted beans or grains between the bread slices.

Crustless spinach pie

SERVES 2

1 ½ lb (700 g) spinach, chopped
oil
1 onion, chopped
pinch dill seeds
bunch parsley, chopped
pinch nutmeg
pinch cumin
freshly ground black pepper

wheatgerm
4 oz (100 g) ricotta
4 oz (100 g) fetta, crumbled
2 eggs
4 oz (100 g) hard cheese, grated
4 rashers lean bacon, chopped
    (optional)

Steam the spinach lightly. Drain in a sieve, pressing out all excess liquid.

Oil a non-stick frying-pan and sauté the onion. Add the dill seeds and toss in the pan until they change colour. Add the parsley and seasoning.

Oil a large, deep pie-plate and sprinkle on enough wheatgerm to coat it thoroughly. Shake off any excess wheatgerm into a bowl. In the same bowl combine the ricotta, fetta and onion mixture.

Spread the spinach in the wheatgerm-coated pie-plate. Cover the spinach with the cheese mixture. Whisk the eggs thoroughly with half the hard cheese. Pour over the ricotta and spinach. If using bacon, add on top of the egg mixture at this stage. Sprinkle the remaining grated cheese over and bake at 350°F/180°C/Gas 4 for 30–40 minutes until the eggs are set.

CHAPTER TWO

Protein power

Before the rediscovery of fibre, nutritionists and dieticians were constantly at pains to stress the need for adequate protein in our diets – indeed, they may have over-stressed its importance. Protein is an essential constituent of all living cells, vital for rebuilding body tissue, creating energy, promoting growth and protecting the body against infection. Yet much recent research in the field of nutrition indicates that we do not need as much protein as we may have been led to believe.

According to some experts the average diet contains about twice as much as protein as is necessary for the body's requirements, and most of this comes from animal sources, which are also high in saturated fats. We should aim to cut the amount of protein in half, and to ensure that about 70 per cent of that is derived from vegetable sources. Ideally, the remaining 30 per cent animal protein should be derived mainly from fish, game, fowl, eggs, low-fat dairy products and, minimally, trimmed red meats.

Proteins are chemical compounds built up from units of fatty acids called amino acids, of which there are twenty-two. The body can manufacture all but eight amino acids; these eight 'essential' amino acids must be supplied from the diet. Some foods are described as being 'complete' proteins (for example, lean meat, fish, skimmed milk and eggs) in that they contain all the eight essential amino acids. 'Incomplete' proteins (for example, wholegrains and legumes) contain some of the essential amino acids. Complete proteins can be obtained in the diet by combining incomplete proteins. For example, the incomplete protein combination found in a wholemeal peanut-butter sandwich fulfils a large male's protein requirement for an entire 24-hour period.

As complementary proteins, amino acids from grains and legumes balance each other out to make a whole protein. Other cheap and easily obtainable sources of protein include potatoes and cereals. Legumes (beans, peas and lentils, etc.) also yield a high percentage of protein weight for weight that complements potatoes and cereals. If you were to add to this some leaf vegetables and essential fats to provide some relief for the taste buds, and essential nutrients such as other vitamins and minerals, you would have a high-quality basic diet – one which is unfortunately a far cry from most people's.

Meat

During the last few decades meat consumption has risen and so too has the incidence of digestive complaints, as well as of heart disease and cancer. This inevitably raises questions concerning the meat content of our diets. Could it be that because cooking destroys enzymes in flesh, cooked meat cannot be efficiently broken down by our digestive systems? The more meat is cooked to render it safe to eat, the more indigestible it becomes. As waste matter in our systems, our bodies cannot eliminate it efficiently and this waste matter becomes toxic in the bowel. Eating meat in a raw state is of course no answer, as parasites could remain in the tissue.

A further problem arises because factory-bred animals are treated with hormones and their feedstuffs contain many additives which are undesirable for humans. Some of these substances must remain in the tissue of the animal when it is slaughtered and are consequently still there when we eat it. It would not be considered safe for humans to ingest them if they were administered in any other way. How, then, can we assume that it is safe to eat the animals that have eaten them?

Meat also contains high levels of uric acid, the by-product of protein digestion. The amount of uric acid that accumulates as a result of eating a large quantity of meat is greater than that which can be eliminated from the body. Such a high level of toxins can lead to a deterioration in health. Some experts have suggested that a gap of two days should be maintained between meals with a high meat content to ensure that the majority of toxins are dispersed. Otherwise, a regular supply of fresh fruits, vegetable juices and yoghurt will help keep uric acid levels down.

The liver and kidneys can deal with quite high levels of uric acid, but the toxic build-up in the digestive tract can combine with other toxic elements and travel to the body cells. Adrenalin, from the meat, can pass into the bloodstream and not only stimulate the adrenal glands but cause over-stimulation of the thyroid too.

Another problem with meat is its calorie content, which can create, or contribute to, a weight problem. A lean piece of ham may comprise 25 per cent protein and 75 per cent fat. Lean steak is about 65 per cent protein, 35 per cent fat: mostly saturated fat.

One way to cut down on meat consumption is to reduce the quantities specified in recipes, and thus save money as well as improving your diet. Traditional cookbooks tend to stipulate about 8 oz (225 g) meat per person. Many of the recipes in this book enable you to provide four helpings with that amount of meat, without anyone feeling deprived.

Other protein foods

Recent American research suggests that the body needs only 37 grams of protein a day. If this is so, 800 grams (less than 2 lb) spinach could provide our daily protein needs. Few people would want to eat that much spinach every day, but the point to note is how valuable a role spinach can play in the average diet. Spinach and lentils have a natural affinity and complement each other well. Many ethnic dishes, in particular, use them in combination to provide delicious dishes which have the bonus of being nutritionally well balanced.

Several of the recipes in this book utilize spinach, but please note that while for most people this vegetable is a valuable toxin-eliminator, some people cannot tolerate its oxalic acid content and should therefore restrict their consumption.

Wholegrains are an ideal source of protein – and, of course, of fibre. Apart from being inexpensive, they make excellent balanced meals in combination with other foods. Wheat, rice and other cereals all feature in the recipes that follow, which include both simple dishes for everyday meals and more elaborate ones suitable for entertaining.

Other high-fibre protein foods are pulses and legumes. Coupled with grains they form complementary proteins making complete amino acid chains similar to those found in eggs and meats.

Following a healthier, wholefood regime does not mean giving up meat. Among the recipes in this book are a good number that incorporate lean meats, and they prove what good results can be achieved with very little meat.

Fish, one of the healthier sources of proteins, is also featured. White fish (for example, cod or haddock) has about 70 calories per 4 oz (100 g). It comprises 81 per cent water, 17.5 per cent protein, 1.25 per cent vitamins and minerals and only 0.25 per cent fat. It does not contain any carbohydrate or fibre. Oily fish (for example, herring or mackerel) has 68 per cent protein, 13.5 per cent fat, which is polyunsaturated, and 1.25 per cent vitamins and minerals (including niacin and vitamin D, which are absent from white fish). It has less cholesterol than either meat or shellfish, no carbohydrate or fibre and 200 calories per 4 oz (100 g).

Shellfish does contain a little carbohydrate. For example, scallops have about 4 per cent and oysters 5 per cent. They are high in protein, iron, calcium, riboflavin and niacin, contain about 3 per cent fat and are comparatively high in cholesterol. Lobster and prawns have twice as much cholesterol as red meat, oysters even more.

It goes without saying that serving fish deep-fried and coated in batter counteracts completely its nutritious attributes.

Some recent research has shown that fish oils are beneficial to sufferers from heart disease. Whether or not this includes you, you will find some unusual and tempting fish recipes to try among those that follow.

Boiled black-bean bread

8oz (225g) black beans, cooked
8oz (225g) wholemeal flour
3 teaspoons (15ml) baking powder
2 large eggs

3 tablespoons (45ml) or more skimmed
  milk
1 tablespoon (15ml) vegetable oil

Oil a basin or brioche mould well. Beat up the beans, ideally in a food processor. Mix the flour and baking powder in a large bowl. Beat together the eggs, milk and oil. Stir into the flour and add the beans. Beat well, adding a little more milk to obtain a soft mixture. Turn into the oiled container and cover with a lid or foil.

In a large saucepan bring enough water to the boil to come half-way up the side of the basin. Put the basin in the water, bring back to the boil, cover and simmer for about 2½ hours, topping up with boiling water if necessary. Test with a cooking skewer, which should come out moist but clean. Allow bread to cool for about 10 minutes in basin, then turn out on to a wire rack. Cut into slices to serve.

Note Bean bread recipes from the Boston area of the USA contain sugar. For a sweet result add 1 tablespoon (15 ml) molasses with the egg. Alternatively, for a different colour and texture try using kidney, lima or pinto beans instead of black beans.

Sprouted soya bread

Sprouted beans are a valuable source of vitamins. The vitamin C content of soya beans increases by more than 500 per cent by the third day of sprouting. There are also significant increases in the level of B vitamins, vitamin E and protein.

½ teaspoon (2.5ml) brown sugar
¼ pint (150 ml) warmed water
2 teaspoons (10ml) dried yeast

2 tablespoons (30ml) sprouted soya beans
12oz (35g) wholemeal flour
sesame seeds

Dissolve the sugar in the water. Sprinkle the yeast on the water and leave in a warm place to become frothy (about 15–20 minutes depending on the temperature). Gently mix the soya beans with the flour. Mix in the yeast mixture. Put the mixing bowl in a warm place for the dough to double in size (about 40 minutes).

Knock the dough back and knead well. Turn into an oiled loaf-tin. Leave to rise a second time. The dough should reach the top of the tin. Sprinkle with sesame seeds, then bake at 400°F/200°C/Gas 6 for about 30 minutes until the loaf is brown, well risen and sounds hollow when tapped on the bottom.

Wholemeal crumpets

Crumpets are ideal for breakfast, afternoon tea or snacks at any time. Eaten hot on their own, topped with low-fat spread or toasted with tomatoes, they are an excellent alternative source of protein. And these wholemeal crumpets are not only easy to make, high in fibre and additive-free: they are a great improvement on the supermarket version.

MAKES ABOUT 12

1 teaspoon (5ml) dried yeast
5 fl oz (150ml) warm water
¼ teaspoon (1ml) vitamin C powder
6oz (175g) wholemeal flour

pinch vegetable seasoning
1 teaspoon (5ml) baking powder
6 fl oz (175ml) warmed milk
oil

Add the dried yeast to the warm water in a jug and sprinkle on the vitamin C. Leave in a warm place for about 15 minutes until frothy. In a large bowl mix the flour, vegetable seasoning and baking powder. Make a well in the centre and add the yeast mixture. Add the milk. Beat well to a batter-like consistency (a good 5 minutes: the texture of the finished crumpets relies on this stage). Cover and leave in a warm place for 1 hour until the mixture is sponge-like. Beat again for another 3 minutes. Add a little more warmed liquid at this stage if the consistency is too thick.

Prepare a frying-pan, preferably non-stick, by oiling lightly. Also oil four crumpet rings – again, preferably non-stick, for these need only initial light oiling. Heat the pan to hot for a minute, then slightly reduce the heat.

Pour enough batter into the crumpet ring to fill to a depth of ½ inch (1 cm). Cook until the crumpet is set and the surface begins to dry. Remove the rings and flip over the crumpets. Cook for just 30 seconds on the other side to produce the characteristic pale golden colour. Cool on a wire rack. When required, warm under the grill.

Crunchy peanut bread

¼ pint (150ml) low-fat milk
1 teaspoon (5ml) honey
2 teaspoons (10ml) dried yeast
4oz (100g) peanuts, chopped or
    roughly ground

12oz (350g) wholemeal flour
pinch sesame-seed salt
1 egg, whisked

Heat the milk to lukewarm. Remove from the heat and add the honey and yeast. Leave in a warm place until foaming. Combine the nuts and flour with the sesame-seed salt. Add the egg and yeast mixture. Beat well. With certain types of flour a little more liquid may be necessary to achieve a moist dough: a couple of spoonfuls of warmed water should be sufficient. Oil a loaf-tin, turn the dough into it and smooth the surface. Bake at 325°F/160°C/Gas 3 for 1–1¼ hours until cooked. Cool for 5 minutes, then turn out on to a wire rack.

Peanut croquettes

8 oz (225 g) wholemeal breadcrumbs

2 oz (50 g) wheatgerm

4 oz (100 g) peanuts, finely ground

4 oz (100 g) Swiss cheese, grated

¼ pint (150 ml) low-fat milk

2 oz (50 g) fine oats

Combine all the ingredients except the oats. Shape into 'sausages' about 1 inch (2.5 cm) round and 2 inches (5 cm) long, so that they just fit into your hand. Roll into the oats. Place on an oiled baking tray and bake at 350°F/180°C/Gas 4 for 20 minutes until brown. For a crisper all-over finish, turn once. Eat warm or cold.

If made slightly smaller these croquettes are ideal for dipping into garlicky home-made mayonnaise-based dips.

Cabbage nut korma

SERVES 4

2 large onions, chopped

4 cloves garlic, crushed

4 oz (100 g) peanuts, roughly
   chopped

2 teaspoons (10 ml) cumin seeds

1 tablespoon (15 ml) ground
   coriander

1 teaspoon (5 ml) mustard seeds,
   crushed

1 tablespoon (15 ml) garam masala

1 tablespoon (15 ml) olive oil

2 potatoes, scrubbed and cut into
   eighths

4 oz (100 g) mushrooms,
   quartered

8 oz (225 g) cabbage, shredded
   (ideally white Dutch or Savoy)

4 tomatoes, chopped

4 fl oz (100 ml) tomato juice

2 oz (50 g) ground almonds

4 fl oz (100 ml) natural low-fat
   yoghurt

Sauté the onions, garlic, nuts and spices together. Add the potatoes and cook gently until they soften. Add the mushrooms and cabbage. Stir. Add the tomatoes and juice. Add the ground almonds. Cook for a further 10 minutes. Stir in the yoghurt, to taste, and sprinkle with more garam masala if liked. When the potatoes are thoroughly cooked serve with brown rice.

Levant filo

4 oz (100 g) lean beef, minced

1 small onion, chopped

1 teaspoon (5 ml) oregano

2 tablespoons (30 ml) pine nuts

1 tomato, chopped

1 tablespoon (15 ml) tomato purée

good shake freshly ground black
   pepper mixed with 1 teaspoon
   (5 ml) cinnamon

1 oz (25 g) sultanas soaked in
   2 tablespoons (30 ml) fruit juice
   (e.g. apple, grape or orange)

2 large eggs, separated

4 fl oz (100 ml) natural low-fat
   yoghurt

8 oz (225 g) filo pastry

2 oz (50 g) polyunsaturated
   margarine, melted

4 oz (100 g) fetta cheese, grated

3 oz (75 g) flaked almonds

In a non-stick frying-pan brown the mince well, making sure it is well broken up. Add the onion and brown. Add the oregano, nuts and tomato. When well cooked, mix in the tomato purée and a pinch of the mixed pepper seasoning. The mixture should be dry and the fat cooked off. There should be no sauce.

Add the sultanas. Whisk the egg yolks with the yoghurt and combine with the meat mixture. Whisk the egg whites and fold in. Carefully unfold the filo pastry and lay one sheet across the base of a well oiled rectangular non-stick baking dish. Brush the pastry sheet with melted margarine and place another on top. Place a third layer on top of that and brush with margarine.

Spread a third of the meat mixture on the pastry. Sprinkle with cheese and almonds. Repeat the process until all the mixture is used up. Sprinkle the top layer with the remainder of the nuts. Bake at 425°F/220°C/Gas 7 for 5 minutes then reduce the heat to 375°F/190°C/Gas 5 and cook for a further 45 minutes or until crisp and golden.

To ensure that the dish is cooked lift the pastry with a metal egg slice and leave it, propped, for a further 10 minutes at 300°F/150°C/Gas 2.

Cut into squares and serve warm.

Cooking grains and beans

The cooking times given in the recipes for plainly prepared boiled grains and beans may err on the side of caution, because as grains and beans have increased in popularity and their turnover in food retail outlets has speeded up they are reaching the consumer in a far less dried-out state than was the case only a couple of years ago. For example, small beans used to need a full hour's boiling; now, as long as they *do* boil, they may well cook in half the time. It is very important that the beans are fully cooked, but if they are over-cooked they will break up and become mushy. Experience with these ingredients is the best guide.

Dried pasta, for example, keeps almost indefinitely. As a rule wholegrain products take longer to cook than refined ones, but wholemeal tagliatelle, a comparatively new product, will probably take the same time (or even less) to cook than a white macaroni which has been around, in the warehouse or retail outlet, a while and therefore had longer in which to dry out.

Vacuum-flask preparation Apart from boiling beans and grains in water or stock you can also prepare them for cooking with other ingredients using a vacuum flask or jug. Bring a scant pint (600ml) water to the boil. Measure 2oz (50g) grain or beans into 1-pint (½-litre) flask, top up with water leaving a small gap at the top, screw on the stopper and leave overnight. The next day, tip out, drain and proceed with the recipe.

It is advisable to check that beans have boiled for at least 10 minutes at some stage during the cooking process to ensure that they are fully digestible. Beans that appear to be cooked may still harbour toxins unless these have been destroyed by the boiling process. Particular care is needed, for this reason, with red kidney beans. A great deal of the reputation beans suffer for being indigestible or causing flatulence has resulted from people eating undercooked beans.

Black-bean soup

SERVES 4

8oz (225g) black beans, washed and soaked
2½ pints (1.4 litres) vegetable stock
1 small onion, chopped
2 tablespoons (30ml) olive oil
1 small carrot, chopped
1 stalk celery, chopped
1 bay leaf
1 small potato, chopped
1 teaspoon (5ml) oregano
1 tablespoon (15ml) fresh parsley, chopped
freshly ground black pepper
2 tablespoons (30ml) lemon juice
fresh lemon slices

Place the beans in a saucepan with the stock and cook for 2 hours or until soft. Alternatively, pressure-cook until soft.

Sauté the onion in the oil, and add the rest of the vegetables and herbs. Stir. Add to the beans and cook for a further half hour until all is amalgamated. Add the lemon juice.

Serve in bowls, each topped with lemon slice.

Granary French stick is an ideal accompaniment for this soup.

Crusty field casserole

SERVES 4

8 oz (225 g) English field or brown
   foul beans, cooked
8 oz (225 g) corn kernels
3 tomatoes, sliced
1 onion, chopped
4 stalks celery, chopped
1 clove garlic, crushed
generous sprinkling thyme and
   summer savory

pinch cayenne pepper
8 oz (225 g) brown rice, cooked
1 tablespoon (15 ml) tomato
   purée
½ pint (300 ml) stock
2 oz (50 g) low-fat hard cheese
1 tablespoon (15 ml) wheatgerm

Combine in a bowl the beans, corn, tomatoes, onion, celery, herbs and pepper.

Spread half the rice in a casserole dish. Cover with the vegetable and bean mixture. Mix the tomato purée into the stock. Cover the bean mixture with the remainder of the rice and pour over the stock. Mix the cheese and wheatgerm together and sprinkle over the rice.

Bake, uncovered, at 350°F/180°C/Gas 4 for 30 minutes.

Bean loaf

This is a very versatile and adaptable recipe. The basic recipe given below produces a soft, pâté-like consistency. Many of the ingredients are optional. For example, you could omit the tahini and mushrooms, perhaps adding mushroom ketchup instead. A little miso (about 2 teaspoons/10 ml) will produce a delicious but much darker finished loaf.

8 oz (225 g) light beans, soaked (e.g.
   lima, mung or flageolet)
3 carrots
2 large sticks of celery
6 mushrooms
1 onion

2 oz (50 g) ground sesame seeds
2 oz (50 g) wholemeal flour
2 tablespoons (30 ml) tahini
soy sauce (or miso) to taste
about ¼ pint (150 ml) water,
   vegetable juice or stock

Cook the beans in plenty of boiling water.

Clean and finely chop (or food-process) the vegetables. Add the beans and seeds. Add the flour. Mix well. Add the tahini and soy sauce. Add enough water or other liquid to form a soft mixture. Turn into a 1-lb oiled loaf-tin, smooth the surface and bake at 300°F/150°C/Gas 2 for about 45 minutes or until the loaf is firm.

When cooked, leave the loaf in the loaf-tin to cool for a while, then turn out on to a serving plate. Serve surrounded with home-made coleslaw.

Corn crêpes

4 oz (100 g) corn meal
pinch baking powder
1 egg, beaten

½ pint (300 ml) buttermilk
1 tablespoon (15 ml) oil

Mix together all the ingredients to form a fine batter.

Lightly oil a non-stick crêpe pan. Pour in enough batter to cover. Cook the crêpe on one side. Flip over and cook the other.

To serve, top with chilli, salad, guacamole, grated cheese, corn kernels in tomato sauce and/or yoghurt. Cover the topping with grated low-fat cheese and melt under the grill.

Bran sesame crackers

3 oz (75 g) fine-ground oatmeal
1½ oz (40 g) bran
4 oz (100 g) wholemeal flour
4 tablespoons (60 ml) polyunsatu-
* rated margarine or oil*

1 tablespoon (15 ml) honey (for
* sweet flavour) or 1 teaspoon*
* (5 ml) vegetable seasoning (for savoury)*
¼ pint (150 ml) low-fat skimmed milk
3 oz (75 g) sesame seeds, toasted

Combine the first six ingredients in a food processor or mixer. Add in half the sesame seeds.

Roll out the dough as thinly as possible. Sprinkle the remaining seeds on top and roll in. Place the dough on an oiled baking sheet and score into squares (about 16).

Bake in a pre-heated oven at 350°F/200°C/Gas 4 for 10–12 minutes. Remove from the oven and loosen the biscuit slightly. Leave to firm up. Break into squares. Store in an airtight tin.

Oat flan pastry

This pastry is particularly suitable for quiches.

3½ oz (90 g) rye flour
1½ oz (40 g) oats

2 fl oz (50 ml) oil
2 tablespoons (30 ml) water

Combine all the ingredients, adding only enough water for the mixture to hold together.

Lightly oil a medium non-stick pie-plate and press the mixture into it. Prick the bottom with a fork and bake at 425°F/220°C/Gas 7 for 12 minutes until crisp and golden. The pie crust is now ready for filling.

High-fibre meat loaf

SERVES 6

1 onion, chopped	1 pint (600ml) tomato juice
1 clove garlic	1lb (450g) lean beef, minced
1 stick celery	3oz (75g) oatmeal
1 carrot	freshly ground black pepper
4oz (100g) courgettes	worcestershire sauce
2oz (50g) fresh parsley	1 egg

Finely chop or food-process the vegetables and herbs, without allowing them to become mushy. Mix in the tomato juice. In a bowl combine the meat, vegetables, oatmeal and seasonings, plus a couple of shakes of worcestershire sauce. Beat in the egg. Turn the mixture into a loaf-tin. Place the tin in a water bath and bake for 1–1¼ hours at 350°F/180°C/Gas 4 until cooked.

Triple-cooked wheat

SERVES 2 AS A MAIN COURSE, 4 AS A SIDE DISH

½lb (225g) wheat berries	2 tablespoons (30ml) soy sauce (to taste)
1 pint (600ml) water	pinch five-spice powder
1 onion, cut into segments and separated	freshly ground black pepper
	bunch watercress to garnish
2 tablespoons (30ml) sesame-seed oil	
2 carrots, cut on the bias	

Toast the wheat berries in a dry frying-pan until they begin to brown and smell nutty (about 5–8 minutes). Bring 1 pint (600ml) water to the boil and simmer the berries in it for about 1–1½ hours. When cooked, drain, but retain the cooking water.

Sauté the onion in the oil, add the carrots and cook until just tender. Add the wheat and stir-fry for a further 5 minutes. Add the soy sauce, five-spice powder, pepper and about 4 tablespoons (60ml) of the cooking water. Cook for a further 5 minutes.

Turn into a serving dish and garnish with sprigs of watercress round the edges.

Shredded vegetables such as cabbage and capsicum can be made more interesting by adding in chillis and limes.

Potato pie crust

This is a 'different' pastry with a good flavour and texture
for use in savoury pies.

1 oz (25 g) low-fat spread
2 oz (50 g) mashed potatoes
2 oz (50 g) low-fat hard cheese,
  grated

2 oz (50 g) oat flakes
4 oz (100 g) wholemeal flour
1 teaspoon (2.5 ml) lemon juice
water to mix

Cream the fat and potatoes together. Mix in the cheese, oats and flour. Mix
into the potatoes. Add the lemon juice and enough cold water to form a stiff
dough. Roll out and use as pie crust.

Depending on the filling ingredients, bake at 350°F/180°C/Gas 4 for about
30 minutes.

Potato dosas

Dosas are frequently served to accompany Indian meals, especially
breakfast. They are very good topped with grilled tomatoes or beans,
or even yoghurt.

6 oz (180 g) cold, cooked potatoes,
  mashed
6 oz (180 g) wholemeal flour
2 tablespoons (30 ml) olive oil, or
  sunflower oil

freshly ground black pepper
1 teaspoon (5 ml) garam masala
other spices and herbs to taste

Mix the potatoes into the flour, working with your hands to form a good
smooth dough. Work in the oil and seasonings. Add (or omit) the other
spices and herbs according to taste. Press out the dough as flat as possible
on a floured surface. Then roll thinly to a maximum of ⅛ inch (2.5 mm). Cut
into four large rounds about 6 inches (15 cm) in diameter (perhaps using a
saucepan lid). Dry-fry in a non-stick frying-pan until the dosas are browned
and crisped on both sides. Flip the dosas over several times during frying to
cook on both sides.

Dosas are best served immediately. Alternatively, they can be prepared
in advance and re-heated in the oven, or eaten cold.

*A tomato salad arranged in the round with raw mushrooms, olives, onions and cress
makes either a good starter, dressed with cold pressed olive oil, or a colourful
accompaniment to a grain-based main course.*

Basic millet pilaff

4 oz (100 g) millet
1 tablespoon (15 ml) olive oil
2 cloves garlic, chopped
1 onion, chopped

2 carrots, scrubbed and sliced
1 pint (600 ml) stock
freshly ground black pepper
sprinkling of chervil

Sauté the millet in the oil, then add the garlic and onion. Add the carrots and stir. Add the stock and bring to the boil. Simmer for 40 minutes until the liquid has been absorbed and the millet has doubled in volume. Stir in the seasonings and serve.

Paella

This is a classic example of how in ethnic cuisines grains are combined with a little meat protein to extend and balance the dish. The finished dish, low in fat but high in fibre and other nutrients, would do justice to any dinner party. Compared with the cost of a similarly impressive meat dish it is also inexpensive, despite the use of prawns.

SERVES 6

8 oz (225 g) brown rice
2 tablespoons (30 ml) olive oil
2 chicken breasts, cut into bite-sized chunks
2 onions, sliced
4 cloves garlic, crushed
1 red pepper, diced
1 green pepper, diced

1 lb (500 g) white fish, boned and cut into pieces
8 oz (225 g) prawns, peeled, plus a few whole for garnish
4 tomatoes, cut into segments
strands of saffron steeped in 1½ pints (900 ml) hot water or low-salt vegetable stock
olives to garnish

Wash and cover the brown rice with water. Leave to soak. In a paella pan sauté the chicken in half the oil until it begins to brown well. Turn down the heat and add the rest of the oil and onions. Sauté until the onions are golden. Add the garlic and peppers. Stir. Add the fish. Drain the rice, add to the pan and mix. Add the prawns, tomatoes and hot water or stock. Bring to the boil and cook until the rice has absorbed the water. Alternatively, cover the casserole and bake in the oven at 350°F/180°C/Gas 4 for the equivalent length of time (about 40 minutes). The dish is ready when the rice is tender. Serve straight from the dish, garnished with olives.
Note Traditionally this dish is made with chicken joints complete with skin and bone, but the dish will contain much less fat if the skin is removed. Both

cooked mussels (some with shells) and squid can be added for variety; the saffron is essential.

Corn-meal pop-ups

6 oz (180 g) corn meal
2 oz (60 g) wholemeal flour
2 teaspoons (10 ml) baking
    powder

1 tablespoon (15 ml) low-fat Cheddar,
    grated
2 tablespoons (30 ml) safflower oil
8 fl oz (225 ml) buttermilk

Put all the dry ingredients in a bowl. Combine the oil with the buttermilk and mix with the dry ingredients to form a smooth batter. Oil some patty tins well and place empty in the oven, pre-heated to 425°F/220°C/Gas 7. When hot, spoon in the batter until the tins are about two-thirds full. Cook for about 15 minutes until the pop-ups are well-risen and well browned. Cool on a wire rack.

Beef and lentil flan

SERVES 4

6 oz (175 g) split red lentils
1 pint (600 ml) low-fat skimmed milk
1 onion, finely chopped
1 teaspoon (5 ml) ground nutmeg
freshly ground black pepper
12 oz (350 g) lean beef, minced
1 tablespoon (15 ml) worcestershire
    sauce

1 oz (50 g) wholemeal breadcrumbs
1 tablespoon (15 ml) tomato purée
2 cloves garlic, crushed
2 teaspoons (10 ml) French
    mustard
2 eggs, whisked
3 oz (75 g) low-fat Cheddar, grated
parsley

Put the lentils, milk and onion in a saucepan. Bring to the boil. Cover and simmer gently for 1 hour to a thick, mushy consistency. Season with half the nutmeg and black pepper.

Mix the beef with more black pepper and the worcestershire sauce. Combine with the breadcrumbs, tomato purée, the rest of the nutmeg, the garlic and mustard. Add in one whisked egg. Line a 10-inch (25-cm) flan-dish with the meat mixture, pressing it down well and bringing it right up to the edges. Mix the remaining egg into the lentil mixture. Spoon on to the meat base. Sprinkle with the grated cheese and bake at 350°F/180°C/Gas 4 for 45–50 minutes or until the filling has set. Garnish with parsley and serve sliced into wedges.

Lentil slice

SERVES 4

8oz (225g) split red lentils	2 tablespoons (30ml) lemon juice
1 onion, sliced	freshly ground black pepper
1 bay leaf	2oz (50g) low-fat Cheddar, grated
16floz (450ml) water	1 tomato, thinly sliced
1 tablespoon (15ml) olive oil	

Put the lentils, onion, bay leaf, water and most of the oil into a saucepan and bring to the boil. Cook, uncovered, for 20–25 minutes until the lentils are tender and the liquid has been absorbed. Remove the bay leaf. Beat the lemon juice, pepper and half the cheese into the lentils. Use the remaining oil to oil a small, shallow, non-stick baking-tin.

Spoon the lentil mixture into the tin. Smooth the surface. Sprinkle the remaining cheese over the lentils and arrange the tomato slices on top. Bake at 425°F/220°C/Gas 7 for 20 minutes.

Buckwheat and beef

Buckwheat is an excellent grain in nutritional terms. It is less acid-forming than wheat and also contains less carbohydrate. Its 11–15 per cent protein content is higher than that of most other grains, and almost comparable to that found in meat. Buckwheat is also a good source of potassium, while being sodium-free. This recipe calls for 'roasted' buckwheat: the pale variety of buckwheat can easily be toasted in a heavy-based dry frying-pan over a gentle heat until brown, for the same result.

SERVES 4

1lb (450g) beef skirt, sliced	freshly ground black pepper
1 tablespoon (15ml) olive oil	1 tablespoon (15ml) citrus fruit peel,
1 onion, chopped	chopped
4oz (100g) haricot beans, soaked	2 pints (1 litre) vegetable stock
2oz (50g) roasted buckwheat	1 oz (25g) fresh parsley, chopped

In a non-stick frying-pan brown the meat slices in the oil. Add all other ingredients except for the parsley. Transfer to an ovenproof casserole and cook at 300°F/150°C/Gas 2 for 8 hours.

Alternatively, bring the ingredients to the boil, transfer to a crockpot and cook on a low heat for 10 hours.

(If preferred, the meat can be browned without the olive oil in a non-stick frying-pan and the onions added afterwards, but the olive oil combines with the buckwheat to give a good flavour, justifying its addition to what is, after all, a lean cut of meat.)

Serve garnished with the chopped parsley, and accompany with, for example, stir-fried courgettes julienne and chopped tomatoes.

Marinated mango steaks

SERVES 2

1 tablespoon (15 ml) lime juice	*2 fillet steaks*
2 cloves garlic, pressed	*1 tablespoon (15 ml) olive oil*
1 tablespoon (15 ml) ground ginger	*1 small mango*
sprinkling onion powder	*few drops soy sauce*
freshly ground black pepper	*(optional)*

Mix together in a bowl the lime juice, pressed garlic, ginger, onion powder and pepper. Marinate the steaks in this for at least 4 hours. Remove the steaks from the marinade. Reserve the marinade. Heat the oil in a frying-pan and sear the steaks on both sides.

Cut the mango in half, skin and carefully cut off four slices. Reserve these for garnish. Pulp the rest of the fruit. Add to the marinade and add the soy sauce. (For a lower salt content omit the soy sauce.) Add the marinade to the frying-pan and cook until the steaks are ready and the sauce smooth (about 5 minutes).

Serve the steaks in the sauce, garnished with slices of mango.

This dish is good served with carrot and leek stir-fry (page 95).

Green 'fried' lamb chops

SERVES 4

4 loin of lamb chops	*1 tablespoon (15 ml) tarragon*
2 cloves garlic	*2 tablespoons (30 ml) tarragon vinegar*
1 sprig rosemary	*mint*
inner heart summer cabbage, shredded	*freshly ground black pepper*

Trim the fat from the chops. Cut one of the cloves of garlic into slivers and insert into the chops. Fry the chops in a non-stick frying-pan with the rosemary. Chop the remaining garlic. When the chops are cooked remove them from the pan with a slotted spoon, retaining the slivers of garlic and rosemary with the meat. Place the chops on a heated dish and keep warm while the cabbage is prepared. Drain any excess fat from the pan and stir-fry the cabbage with the tarragon for 5 minutes. Add the vinegar and mix. Turn the cabbage on to a warmed serving platter. Arrange the chops on top. Sprinkle with mint and season with black pepper. Serve straight away.

Stuffed pork with cider

SERVES 4

4 large pork chops
STUFFING:
  1 cooking apple, peeled and cored
  8 oz (225 g) natural cottage cheese
  2 heaped tablespoons (good 30 ml)
    fresh wholemeal breadcrumbs
  1 teaspoon (5 ml) salt
  freshly ground black pepper

2 large eating apples
oil
1 large onion, sliced
¾ pint (450 ml) dry cider
4 tablespoons (60 ml) natural
  low-fat yoghurt
1 tablespoon (15 ml) chopped
  parsley

Remove the rind from the pork chops. Pressing the fingertips firmly on the flesh, cut through each chop with a sharp knife parallel to the work-top to make a large pocket for the stuffing.

Grate the cooking apple coarsely and combine with the other stuffing ingredients. Divide the stuffing equally between the chops. With a trussing needle and fine string, or darning needle and thread, sew up the opening of each chop to retain the stuffing during cooking.

Slice the eating apples into ¼-inch (½-cm) rings and cut out the core. Reserve the end pieces and fry in a little oil until golden. Set on an oiled plate and keep warm. Place the chops in a non-stick frying-pan and dry-fry quickly on each side for 3–4 minutes until golden. Add the sliced onion, cider and end slices of apple, chopped.

Cover the frying-pan and cook slowly for 20 minutes, turning the chops once during cooking. The cider should reduce by about half. Stir in the yoghurt. Remove the chops and place on a warmed serving dish. To serve, spoon the sauce over the chops and garnish with the apple rings and a sprinkling of chopped parsley.

Green toad

SERVES 4

8 oz (225 g) spring greens, washed
  and shredded
1 teaspoon (5 ml) savory
8 oz (225 g) lean pork, minced very
  finely
1 teaspoon (5 ml) nutmeg
1 teaspoon (5 ml) ground coriander
1 tablespoon (15 ml) worcestershire
  sauce

1 tablespoon (15 ml) tomato powder
freshly ground black pepper
1 tablespoon (15 ml) oregano
1 onion, chopped
4 eggs, separated
4 tomatoes, sliced
coriander leaves

Put the shredded greens in a non-stick saucepan with the savory and sweat over a low heat until the leaves begin to wilt. Remove from the heat and drain. Combine the meat with the nutmeg, ground coriander, worcestershire sauce, tomato powder, black pepper and oregano. Form the meat into sausage shapes. Cook over a gentle heat in a non-stick frying-pan, and when liquid begins to run out add the onion. Continue to cook until the onion becomes transparent.

Beat the egg yolks in a bowl and add the greens. Beat the egg whites until stiff and add to the greens mixture. Pile into a large oiled casserole dish. Arrange the sausages and onion on the top and place the tomatoes round the edge. Bake at 400°F/200°C/Gas 6 for 30 minutes until the eggy greens rise to form a golden browning round the sausages. Garnish with coriander leaves and serve quickly before the ring collapses.

Noodle eggah

SERVES 6

4 oz (100 g) flat wholemeal noodles	*1 clove garlic, crushed*
4 eggs	*1 tablespoon (15 ml) olive oil*
freshly ground black pepper	*1 chicken fillet, cut on the bias into*
pinch chilli seasoning	*strips*
2 teaspoons (10 ml) paprika	*2 small courgettes,*
2 teaspoons (10 ml) ground cumin	*shredded*
1 small onion, chopped	*coriander leaves to garnish*

Cook the noodles in plenty of boiling water. Drain. Beat the eggs with the seasoning and put to one side.

In a large frying-pan sauté the onion and garlic in the oil. Add the chicken and courgettes. Stir-fry for 5 minutes. Add the noodles and mix well. Add the egg mixture and cook over a gentle heat until the bottom is set. Finish off under the grill. Alternatively, after adding the egg transfer to a casserole and cook in a moderate oven, 350°F/180°C/Gas 4, for 20–30 minutes until the egg is set.

Garnish with coriander leaves and serve cut into wedges.

Macaroni flan

SERVES 4

3 oz (75 g) wholemeal short-cut
   macaroni
small knob low-fat margarine
1 tablespoon (15 ml) low-fat
   skimmed milk
2 tablespoons (30 ml) chervil
1 oz (25 g) parmesan
4 oz (100 g) lean beef, minced
1 onion, chopped
1 clove garlic, crushed
1 stalk celery, finely chopped
2 oz (50 g) cooked lentils

1 small courgette, chopped
4 large mushrooms, sliced
oregano, to taste
freshly ground black pepper
tomato juice
1 egg, whisked
¼ pint (150 ml) natural low-fat
   yoghurt
1 tablespoon (15 ml) mustard
   powder
1 tomato, sliced
2 oz (50 g) low-fat Cheddar, grated

Cook the macaroni in plenty of boiling water. Drain and while warm toss in the margarine, milk, chervil and parmesan. Press the macaroni into the bottom of a well-oiled 10-inch (25-cm) flan-dish.

Sauté the beef in a non-stick frying-pan. Add the onion, garlic and other vegetables and herbs. Season. If the mixture is too dry add tomato juice, as desired. Place the mixture in the macaroni case and smooth the surface.

Beat the egg with the yoghurt and mustard. Pour over the filling. Arrange the tomato slices on top and sprinkle with the cheese. Bake at 350°F/180°C/Gas 4 for 40 minutes until set.

Pizza pie

This is a useful dish for eating cold on picnics or for packed lunches.

SERVES 6

1 teaspoon (5 ml) honey
2 teaspoons (10 ml) dried yeast
7 fl oz (200 ml) warm water
12 oz (350 g) wholemeal flour
1 onion, chopped
2 cloves garlic, crushed
1 tablespoon (15 ml) olive oil
1 lb (450 g) tomatoes, chopped
1 tablespoon (15 ml) basil

1 small green pepper,
   chopped
freshly ground black pepper
pinch chilli seasoning
4 oz (100 g) tuna, cooked
   (alternatively, Italian sausage or
   chorizos)
12 black olives, stoned
1 tablespoon (15 ml) oregano

Mix the honey with the yeast and 3 tablespoons (45 ml) warm water and leave in a warm place to become frothy. Add the yeast mixture to the flour in a bowl. Add the rest of the warm water and mix to form a dough. Knead in the bowl for 5 minutes. Cover and leave in a warm place to rise.

Meanwhile, make the filling. Sauté the onion and garlic in the oil. Add the tomato, basil, green pepper and seasonings. Stir in the tuna and cook until the juice has almost evaporated. Add the olives. Allow to cool. Knead the dough again and divide into two. Roll one piece out into an oblong and line a large, well-oiled, non-stick baking-dish (for example, a swiss-roll tin). Spread the filling evenly over the dough. Roll out the rest of the dough into an oblong to form the lid and place on top of the filling. Pinch the sides and lid together, between the fingers, to seal. Brush the top with a little oil.

Bake at 425°F/220°C/Gas 7 for 30–35 minutes until crisp and golden. On removing from the oven brush the top with a little more oil and sprinkle with basil and oregano.

Browned spaghetti toss

A large non-stick frying-pan, wok or paella pan is the most suitable utensil to use for this dish.

SERVES 4

6oz (175g) wholemeal spaghetti
safflower oil
8oz (225g) smoked haddock fillets,
  cut into small strips
1 bunch spring onions, trimmed and
  chopped
2 tablespoons (30ml) green peas

4 tablespoons (60ml) chopped
  continental parsley
pinch ground fennel seeds
freshly ground black
  pepper
lemon juice to taste
2 eggs, beaten

Cook the spaghetti until tender. Drain well. Put a little into the pan and heat the spaghetti through, ensuring it is well-coated. Increase the heat and add the fish. Toss well for a few minutes until the fish begins to flake. Add the onions, peas and parsley. Sprinkle over the fennel seeds, pepper and lemon juice. Keep the food moving, as in stir-frying.

Remove the pan from the heat and add the eggs. Toss well until all the food is well-coated and the eggs are beginning to cook.

This is good served straight away on a bed of pale, shredded Chinese leaves or crisp lettuce.

Kedgeree

The word kedgeree comes from the Indian word *kichiri*, a dish of rice and lentils. Kedgeree is not itself an authentic Indian dish but it is delicious garnished with fresh coriander leaves and accompanied by a yoghurt raita, served with dosas for brunch or supper.

SERVES 4

olive oil
1 teaspoon (5 ml) dill seeds
1 teaspoon (5 ml) cumin seeds
1 teaspoon (5 ml) mustard seeds
4 cardamoms
1 teaspoon (5 ml) fennel seeds
1 teaspoon fenugreek seeds
4 oz (100 g) brown rice
1 onion, sliced
3 cloves garlic, chopped
1 small green pepper, sliced

4 oz (100 g) brown lentils, cooked
(retaining any water)
1 tablespoon (15 ml) fish masala (see page 77)
2 fresh fillets (e.g. smoked haddock, smoked mackerel, fresh herrings)
few methi leaves
freshly ground black pepper
pinch vegetable seasoning
lemon juice
4 hard-boiled eggs

Grease a large non-stick frying-pan sparingly with the oil. Add all the spice seeds and heat until they begin to pop. Reduce the heat a little and add the rice. Cook until the rice is opaque and a toasted spice smell comes off the pan. Add the onion and garlic. Continue cooking until the onions soften and begin to brown. Add the green pepper. Add the lentils and any residual cooking water. Add the fish masala. Add the fish fillets, and enough additional water to cover the contents of the pan. Add the methi leaves.

Bring to the boil and continue to cook until the rice is done and the water has been absorbed (about 40 minutes). Season with black pepper and vegetable seasoning. Add a little lemon juice. Slice and quarter the hard-boiled eggs and add to the pan. Heat through and serve.

This dish can be cooked in advance and left off the heat in the pan until required. To serve, heat through gently and thoroughly, adding a little more liquid if necessary.

To vary, add a different kind of dahl: split peas, for example. Alternatively, for a very colourful dish, use a red pepper with green mung beans instead of a green pepper with brown lentils.

Crescent fish

This dish makes a good snack, or first course for a dinner party.

SERVES 8

4 oz (100 g) polyunsaturated
  margarine
4 oz (100 g) curd cheese
4 oz (100 g) wholemeal flour
4 oz (100 g) cooked or canned sardines

1 tablespoon (15 ml) lemon juice
½ teaspoon (2.5 ml) garam masala
freshly ground black pepper
1 small onion, minced
1 tablespoon (15 ml) minced parsley

Combine the margarine, cheese and flour in a food processor or mixer. Beat until a stiff dough is formed. Chill the dough for 1 hour. If using canned sardines drain well. Mash the sardines with lemon juice, spices, onion and parsley. Roll out the dough into a large oblong and divide it into about 4 squares. Cut each square in half to form two triangles. Place a spoonful of the fish mixture in the centre of each triangle. Roll up from the long side towards the point as if making a croissant. Pinch the ends and curve them in slightly to form a crescent. Arrange the crescents, with space between them, on a lightly oiled non-stick baking tray. Chill in the refrigerator for about 10 minutes to firm up. Bake at 450°F/230°C/Gas 8 for 10 minutes or until golden brown.

Ring of fish

SERVES 4

1 lb (450 g) plaice fillets, skinned
2 oz (50 g) brown crabmeat
3 eggs
6 tablespoons (90 ml) natural low-
  fat yoghurt
1 pint (600 ml) low-fat skimmed milk
2 oz (50 g) brown rice, cooked

freshly ground black pepper
½ oz (12.5 g) margarine
2 oz (50 g) wholemeal flour
1 teaspoon (5 ml) lemon juice
2 tablespoons (30 ml) chopped
  parsley
2 tablespoons (30 ml) dill

Cut the fish fillets into broad, flat strips and use them to line a medium-sized, well-oiled ring mould. Liquidize together the crabmeat, eggs, yoghurt and half the milk. Stir in the cooked rice. Season. Pour the mixture into the lined mould. Cover with foil. Place in a baking dish half-filled with water. Bake at 325°F/170°C/Gas 3 for about 1 hour until just set.

  Make up a white sauce with the remaining milk, margarine and flour. Add the lemon juice and herbs. When cooked, turn the fish ring out on to a warmed plate. Drain off any excess liquid. Pour some of the sauce into the centre, allowing some to trickle over the mould.

Fish patties

These 'up market' fish cakes are very simple to make and very tasty.
Minced fish is an ideal way to introduce fish into the diet of those who
like its flavour but are put off by the bones and skin.
(Many fishmongers will mince fish for you.)

SERVES 2

8oz (225g) white fish, minced
tarragon leaves
dill weed
freshly ground black pepper
4 tablespoons (100g) dried potato, or
   about 4 medium potatoes, cooked
   and dry

1 onion, chopped
1 tablespoon (15ml) tomato purée
sprinkling oats
oil

In a non-stick frying-pan sauté the fish until it becomes opaque. Add the
herbs and pepper to taste. Keep the fish moving during cooking, as
minced fish is inclined to stick.

Either make up the dried potato or beat the cooked potatoes until they
are mashed and smooth. Add the onion and mix. Add the fish and mix.
Add the tomato purée. If the mixture is too soft to handle, add oatflakes
and leave in a refrigerator for a while to firm up.

Lightly oil a non-stick frying-pan. Using your hands, form the fish
mixture into four balls and flatten into patties. Brown on both sides. Serve
straight away or keep warm in the oven.

The tomato purée may be replaced by a couple of fresh tomatoes
prepared with the onion in a food processor. The cakes are tasty re-heated
in the oven the next day.

Note that 'patty' can become 'kofta' by the addition of spices such as
garlic, cumin, coriander and ginger.

Crab pilaff

SERVES 4

4oz (100g) brown rice
1 onion, chopped
2 cloves garlic, chopped
1 tablespoon (15ml) oil
1 teaspoon (5ml) ground turmeric
1 teaspoon (5ml) ground paprika
1 small green pepper, chopped
2oz (50g) broad beans (or peas)

2 tomatoes, chopped
8oz (225g) crabmeat (brown, white
   or mixed)
7floz (200ml) stock
2 tablespoons (30ml) sherry
1 tablespoon (15ml) dill
   seeds
freshly ground black pepper

Soak the rice in water for a couple of hours before preparing the dish. Rinse and drain the rice.

Sauté the onion and garlic in the oil in a non-stick frying-pan. Add the spices and cook for about 5 minutes. Add the rice, the remainder of the vegetables and the tomatoes. Sauté for about 10 minutes. Add the crabmeat and stock with the sherry. Season. Bring to the boil. Reduce the heat and simmer, covered, for about 40 minutes. Serve hot with steamed asparagus.

Tuna mousse

SERVES 4 AS A STARTER

1 tablespoon (15 ml) vegetable
    setting agent
¼ pint (150 ml) dry white wine
8 oz (225 g) tuna, cooked
¼ pint (150 ml) natural low-fat
    yoghurt
2 tablespoons (30 ml) fine oatmeal
1 tablespoon (15 ml) tarragon
    vinegar

1 teaspoon (5 ml) tarragon
1 very small onion, grated or minced
1 teaspoon (5 ml) lemon juice
8 slices tomato
few drops Tabasco sauce
freshly ground black pepper
dill weed or basil leaves to garnish

Mix the setting agent with the wine and gently bring to simmering point over a very low heat, stirring all the time. Make sure the powder has dissolved completely. Combine the tuna, yoghurt and oatmeal. Beat well. Beat in the setting mixture, tarragon, onion, lemon juice and Tabasco. Add a generous amount of black pepper. Place one slice of tomato in the bottom of each of four serving dishes. Pour the mousse on top of the tomato slice. Place another tomato slice on top and chill for at least 6 hours to set.

Alternatively, this mousse can be made in one dish. Oil the dish as described above and lay 4 tomato slices on the bottom. Pour the mixture over the top, and place the tomatoes on top, setting them if possible vertically above the first slices. Turn out the four individual mousses. The one-dish mousse is best served scooped out from the bowl.

Garnish with herbs and serve with crusty brown bread.

Coriander cod

2 tablespoons (30 ml) wholemeal
   flour
1 tablespoon (15 ml) ground coriander
freshly ground black pepper
1 lb (450 g) cod or coley, without
   bones or skin, cut into large pieces
oil

lemon juice to taste
2 oz (50 g) oatmeal
¼ pint (150 ml) yoghurt
coriander leaves to garnish
cayenne

Mix together the flour, coriander and pepper. Coat the fish in the seasoned flour. Heat a minimal amount of oil gently in a non-stick frying-pan. Add the fish pieces and sauté for about 10 minutes. Remove the fish to a warmed serving dish in the oven. Add the lemon juice to the frying-pan, blending with any remaining flour. Stir the oatmeal into the yoghurt. Add to the pan and warm through. Pour over the fish. Garnish with coriander. Dust lightly with cayenne, down the centre of the dish, for a colourful finishing touch.

(If the fish is sautéd only briefly to brown, the dish may be kept warm for a short while in a low oven.)

Lentil tuna bake

SERVES 4

6 oz (175 g) red split lentils
freshly ground black pepper
about 4 tablespoons (60 ml) lemon
   juice
oil

1 onion, chopped
8 oz (225 g) tuna fish, cooked
¼ pint (150 ml) natural low-fat
   yoghurt
oatflakes

Place the lentils in a saucepan with 1 pint (600 ml) water. Bring to the boil and simmer for about 20 minutes until the lentils are cooked and most of the liquid has evaporated. Season with pepper and a little of the lemon juice. Put a little oil into a frying-pan and sauté the onion. Add the tuna and season with pepper. Cook until the fish flakes and is well mixed. Place about half the lentils in an oiled pie-dish. Add the tuna mixture.

Whisk the yoghurt with the rest of the lemon juice and pour half over the tuna mixture. Beat the remaining yoghurt mixture into the rest of the lentils and pour over the top of the tuna in the dish. Fork over the top. Sprinkle the top with oatflakes and bake at 375°F/190°C/Gas 5 for about 20 minutes.

Souffléd kippers

SERVES 4

1lb (450g) Jerusalem artichokes, well scrubbed
1oz (25g) polyunsaturated margarine
1 large onion, chopped
¼ pint (150ml) low-fat skimmed milk
1 teaspoon (5ml) chervil
1 teaspoon (5ml) tarragon leaves

freshly ground black pepper
8oz (225g) kipper fillets, cooked
4 eggs, separated
2oz (50g) cream cheese, e.g. Bel Paese
1 tablespoon (15ml) lemon juice
2 tablespoons (30ml) soft wholemeal breadcrumbs

Chop the artichoke into small dice. Melt the margarine in a non-stick frying-pan and sauté the onion slowly until soft. Stir in the artichokes and mix well. Add the milk, herbs and pepper. Bring to the boil, then simmer for 20 minutes, mixing vigorously from time to time so that the artichokes break up and become pulpy.

Flake the kippers, discarding all skin and any remaining bones. Season with black pepper. Beat the egg yolks. Beat the fish, cheese, lemon juice and artichoke mixture into the yolks until smooth. Whisk the egg whites until stiff and carefully fold into the fish mixture. Turn into an oiled 2-pint (1200-ml) soufflé dish, sprinkled with the breadcrumbs. Bake at 375°F/190°C/Gas 5 for 30 minutes. Serve immediately.

Seed-topped fish

SERVES 2

8oz (225g) coley or haddock fillets
4 tomatoes, sliced
1 onion, chopped
1 small green pepper, chopped
freshly ground black pepper
1oz (25g) soft wholemeal breadcrumbs

1oz (25g) low-fat Cheddar, grated
1 teaspoon (5ml) mustard powder
1 lemon, with grated rind and juice
1oz (25g) sunflower seeds, toasted
1 teaspoon (5ml) fennel seeds
dash worcestershire sauce

Oil a shallow casserole. Place the fillets on the bottom. Add the tomatoes, onion and green pepper on top. Season. Mix the breadcrumbs, Cheddar, mustard, lemon rind and sunflower and fennel seeds together. Add the worcestershire sauce and lemon juice. Spread the topping over the fish. Bake at 375°F/190°C/Gas 5 for 20 minutes until crisp and brown on top.

Russian haddock

1½ lb (700g) haddock fillets
freshly ground black pepper
½ pint (300ml) white white
1 tablespoon (15ml)
    polyunsaturated margarine
1 oz (25g) wholemeal flour

1 small green pepper, sliced finely
1 large piece cucumber, cut into
    fat fingers
¼ pint (150ml) natural
    low-fat yoghurt
toasted triangles rye bread

Line a casserole dish with foil. Place the fish in the bottom. Add the pepper and wine and bake in the oven at 350°F/180°C/Gas 4 for 15 minutes. Drain off the liquid and reserve.

Melt the margarine in a saucepan, stir in the flour and add ½ pint (330ml) of the reserved liquid to make a smooth, thickened sauce. Add the green pepper and cucumber to the fish. Add the yoghurt to the sauce and pour over the fish. Return the casserole to the oven for 15 minutes to heat through. Serve garnished with triangles of toasted bread.

For entertaining, sprinkle a spoonful of lumpfish roe over the top as an additional garnish.

Sweetcorn salmon

SERVES 4

1 tablespoon (15ml)
    polyunsaturated margarine
2 tablespoons (30ml) wholemeal
    flour
8 fl oz (225ml) low-fat skimmed milk
freshly ground black pepper

8 oz (225g) salmon, cooked
1 teaspoon (5ml) tarragon
6 oz (175g) sweetcorn kernels,
    cooked
½ soft red pepper, finely
    diced

Melt the margarine in a non-stick saucepan. Stir in the flour. Stir for a few minutes to allow the flour to cook. Add the milk gradually to form a smooth, thick sauce. Season.

Flake the salmon and combine with the tarragon, sweetcorn and red pepper. Add to the sauce and stir. Heat through gently. Transfer to four individual dishes or a small soufflé dish. Serve immediately accompanied by hot chunks of granary bread.

Fresh vegetables, attractively arranged, can easily fit into a dinner-party setting.

Tuna chicken casserole

1 tablespoon (15 ml)
  polyunsaturated margarine
1 onion, chopped
1 chicken breast fillet, skinned,
  boned and chopped
4 oz (100 g) sweetcorn kernels, cooked
8 oz (225 g) tuna, cooked

1 tablespoon (15 ml) wholemeal flour
8 fl oz (225 g) low-fat skimmed milk
2 teaspoons (10 ml) paprika
freshly ground black pepper
1 lb (45 g) spinach, cooked and well drained
3 tablespoons (45 ml) wholemeal
  breadcrumbs

Melt the margarine in a non-stick saucepan and sauté the onion. Add the chicken and brown. Add the sweetcorn and tuna, broken into bite-sized pieces. Cook for 5 minutes. Sprinkle on the flour and stir to mix in. Pour on the milk and bring to the boil. Stir until thickened. Add the paprika and black pepper.

Place the spinach in the bottom of a casserole dish. Pour the chicken mixture on top and sprinkle the surface with the breadcrumbs.

Place in the oven at 400°F/200°C/Gas 6 and bake for 15–20 minutes until the top is crisp and brown and the sauce underneath is bubbling.

Noodles with creamed sauce

2 oz (50 g) lean pork, minced
1 onion, chopped
6 large button mushrooms, finely
  sliced
8 oz (225 g) wholemeal noodles

freshly ground black pepper
¼ pint (500 ml) natural low-fat
  yoghurt
bunch fresh parsley,
  finely chopped

In a non-stick frying-pan sauté the pork until the meat is cooked and every piece is separate. Drain off any excess fat. Add the onion to the pan and cook gently until transparent. Add the mushrooms and cook gently for 5 minutes.

Meanwhile, cook the noodles in plenty of boiled water. Drain.

Add the pork mixture to the drained noodles in a saucepan. Season with pepper. Over a very low heat add the yoghurt. Stir in and heat through. Sprinkle with parsley and serve immediately.

Fresh vegetables cut into julienne strips make a colourful first course. Choose from contrasting ingredients such as mange-tout, carrot, red and green peppers and cauliflower.

Marinated roast pork

This is a very useful dinner-party dish.

SERVES 4

½ lean leg or shoulder of pork,
  trimmed of fat, rolled and boned
½ pint (300 ml) white wine and
  ½ pint (300 ml) cider (or
  1 pint/600 ml apple juice)
4 carrots, scrubbed and sliced
1 large onion, sliced
1 large apple, sliced and cored
2 cloves garlic, sliced
2 sprigs thyme
1 tablespoon (15 ml) coriander seeds
1 tablespoon (15 ml) rubbed sage
6 bay leaves
freshly ground black pepper

Place the pork in a bowl and cover with the wine and cider, or juice, vegetables and spice. Marinate for at least 12 hours or overnight. Remove the pork from the marinade. Reserve the marinade. In a large casserole dish 'dry-fry' the joint until browned all over. Pour off any fat. Pour the marinade over the pork and cook in the oven at 275°F/160°C/Gas 3 for 2½–3 hours until the joint is tender and the liquid much reduced.

To serve, remove the roast to a warmed serving dish. Strain off any fat from the marinade. Remove and liquidize the vegetable and add enough of the liquid to make a smooth sauce. Serve the sauce separately.

Moroccan chicken

SERVES 4

4 chicken joints, boned and skinned
1 large onion, chopped
½ teaspoon (2.5 ml) paprika
½ teaspoon (2.5 ml) ground cumin
freshly ground black pepper
pinch turmeric
a few strands saffron
about 1½ pints (900 ml) stock
  (vegetable cooking water or made
  from a low-salt stock cube)
4 oz (100 g) chick peas, soaked for
  24 hours
1 tablespoon (15 ml) chopped
  coriander
1 sprig lemon thyme
1 tablespoon (15 ml) sultanas,
  soaked
6 oz (175 g) brown rice
2 tablespoons (30 ml) lemon juice
2 tablespoons (30 ml) almond halves

In a non-stick saucepan brown the chicken joints. Add the onion. Stir in the first five spices. Add enough stock to cover. Stir in the chick peas and herbs. Bring to the boil. Add the sultanas, rice and lemon juice. Cover and simmer for 2 hours until the chicken is tender, the chick peas and rice are cooked and the stock is mostly absorbed.

To serve, spoon on to a large serving dish and garnish with almonds.

Red haddock

SERVES 4

1 oz (25 g) wholemeal flour
2 tablespoons (30 ml) paprika
1 lb (450 g) haddock fillets
1 tablespoon (15 ml) olive oil
1 onion, chopped

1 red pepper, sliced
8 fl oz (225 ml) low-fat skimmed milk
4 fl oz (100 ml) stock
freshly ground black pepper
4 oz mushrooms, sliced

Combine the flour and paprika. Coat the fish fillets in the seasoned flour. Heat the oil in a frying-pan and sauté the fillets on each side until cooked (about 8 minutes). Remove and keep warm. Add the onion and red pepper to the frying-pan. Cook through and add in the remaining flour mixture. Mix well and blend in the milk and stock. Season. Stir in the mushrooms and simmer gently, stirring all the time, until a smooth sauce is formed. Pour the sauce on to a serving dish and arrange the fish fillets on top.

Serve with wholemeal noodles.

Baked fish slices

SERVES 4

4 oz (100 g) sardines, cooked, or
cooked mackerel or herring fillet
2 oz (50 g) curd cheese or thickened
natural low-fat yoghurt
sprinkling tarragon
1 oz (25 g) low-fat spread
1 tablespoon (15 ml) tomato purée
freshly ground black pepper

12 slices wholemeal bread from a
small loaf, thinly sliced
4 tomatoes, chopped
3 oz (75 g) low-fat Cheddar, grated
2 eggs
¼ pint (150 ml) low-fat skimmed
milk
red or green pepper rings to garnish

Mash the fish and mix with the curd cheese, tarragon, fat and tomato purée. Season. Spread evenly on the bread slices. Cut each slice into two triangles. Oil a shallow ovenproof dish sparingly.

Arrange a layer of triangles on the bottom of the dish. Add a third of the chopped tomatoes and the grated cheese. Repeat for two more layers until all the bread is used up. Whisk the eggs with the milk and pour over the dish.

Garnish with the pepper rings and bake at 400°F/200°C/Gas 6 for 25–30 minutes until the dish is crisp and brown.

Smoked salmon noodles

This is another ideal dish for dinner parties.

SERVES 4

8oz (225g) wholemeal flat
  noodles
1 small onion, chopped
1 tablespoon (15ml) olive oil
4oz (100g) green peas
1 tablespoon (15ml) poppy seeds
3oz (75g) smoked salmon pieces

3 mushrooms, finely sliced
3 tablespoons (45ml) natural
  low-fat yoghurt
1 avocado, stoned, peeled and sliced
freshly ground black pepper
fresh dill, fennel or tarragon, to
  garnish

Cook the noodles in plain boiling water. Drain. Sauté the onion in the oil, add the peas and seeds and stir until the peas are just beginning to soften. Add the salmon and mushrooms. Stir.

Stir in the yoghurt and noodles and heat through. Distribute the avocado slices through the noodles and season with black pepper. Serve hot.

Garnish with fresh dill, the feathery part of fennel, or tarragon.

Note For a more substantial dish, add hard-boiled egg slices before the avocado.

Fish koftas

MAKES 6

8oz (225g) boned, skinned fish
1 small onion, chopped
2 tablespoons (30ml) oil
2 garlic cloves, crushed
1 small red chilli, chopped
1 teaspoon (5ml) turmeric

1 teaspoon (5ml) ground coriander
1 teaspoon (5ml) ground cumin
1 teaspoon (5ml) mustard seeds,
  roughly crushed
1lb (450g) cold potatoes, mashed
3 tablespoons (45ml) oatmeal

Flake the fish. Sauté the onion in the oil with the garlic. Add the spices and cook until their aroma is released. Mix in the fish. Add the fish, and the potatoes in a bowl and bind together. Break off six small pieces, form into balls and toss in the oatmeal to coat the outsides, throwing the balls gently from hand to hand. Bake in a non-stick baking dish 400°F/200°C/ Gas 6 for 20 minutes. Alternatively, shallow-fry in very little oil for about 10 minutes until the koftas are brown all over.

Fish masala

The recommended fish for this dish is rock salmon, which has few bones and an excellent texture. Two methods are suggested, the first omitting oil altogether (other than the very small amount that is in the fish itself).

SERVES 2

1 teaspoon (5 ml) paprika
1 teaspoon (5 ml) ground coriander
1 teaspoon (5 ml) ground cumin
1 teaspoon (5 ml) garlic powder
1 teaspoon (5 ml) turmeric
1 teaspoon (5 ml) ground fennel seeds
½ teaspoon (2.5 ml) ground cloves
½ teaspoon (2.5 ml) ground cinnamon

½ teaspoon (2.5 ml) ajwan (ideally, or, failing that, thyme)
½ teaspoon (2.5 ml) chilli powder
¼ pint (150 ml) natural low-fat yoghurt
2 tablespoons (30 ml) lime juice
8 oz (225 g) white fish (preferably rock salmon)
dill to garnish

Combine the spices and mix 1½ tablespoons (7.5 ml) of the resulting masala with the yoghurt and lime juice. (Store the rest in a screw-top jar to use as garam masala with other spicy dishes.)

Cut the fish into bite-sized chunks and mix with the yoghurt and masala. Leave to marinate for at least 3 hours. Remove the fish from the marinade using a slotted spoon, and place in an ovenproof dish. Bake at 400°F/200°C/Gas 6 for 15 minutes. Add the marinade to the fish and mix to heat through. Serve garnished with feathery dill.

Alternatively, sauté the fish for 10 minutes in 1 tablespoon (15 ml) olive oil or butter, then add the marinade.

CHAPTER THREE

Hidden extras

Additives and preservatives have begun to give real cause for concern, for practically every manufactured food we buy contains harmful substances of one sort or another. Commercially produced ice cream, for example, often contains ethyl acetate, which is also used as a dry-cleaning fluid; piperonel, also used as an insecticide; amyl acetate, a solvent for oil paint; and propylene glycol, also used in germicides and paint-removers.

Most cured and smoked foods, too, contain toxic fertilizers, introduced by the manufacturers during processing. These poisonous substances have been implicated in cancer by US experts.

What can you do to avoid consuming these unwanted extras?

One answer is to prepare your own charcuterie, which is not only healthier but both cheaper and tastier too. This chapter includes full instructions for smoking and drying food at home as well as a range of ideas for prepared meats, including sausages, pâtés and cheeses.

Pâtés made from vegetables and fish are likely to produce dishes that are lower in fat and higher in vitamins and minerals than rich meat pâtés, and making traditional meat pâtés at home means you can both control the fat content and ensure there are no added preservatives. On the other hand, as you control the ingredients you can always add liver to meat pâtés and thereby introduce valuable vitamin B12, often very low in low-meat diets. (Vegetarians can obtain B12 from vegetable sources such as soya.)

Beef and pork products from delicatessen counters, even plain roast beef slices, are likely to contain potassium nitrate and sodium nitrate as colour preservers, which have been known for at least a decade to be toxic. Potassium nitrate has no preservative qualities but is added to salted meats to encourage an attractive pink colour; it tends to harden meat, and normally sugar is added to counteract this. The nitrate in both potassium nitrate and sodium nitrate combines easily with the amines in food (also those in drugs, alcohol and tobacco smoke) to produce nitrosamines, and these are the compounds which have been found to induce cancer.

The problem is similar for smoked products. In the smoking process foods absorb the coal-tar derivatives which are also known carcinogens. Food can also be brine-cured, but this process adds a high sodium chloride content to the toxins mentioned above. Home curing and smoking produces foods that are entirely devoid of these hazards to health.

The home smoking process is usually carried out using food which has already spent a few days in brine, or has been dried at a steady temperature of 60°F (15°C) for several days. Probably the best items to begin with are small items such as home-made sausages or chicken breast. The object, as in drying, is to remove the moisture from the meat (or fish, vegetables or fruit), and also to introduce additional flavour and preservative qualities.

Drying food to preserve it is very easy. Chillis, citrus peel and mushrooms can all be dried in much the same way as fresh herbs are dried. Chillis, for example, can be threaded on a string through the stem using a trussing needle and hung in a well-ventilated place, away from any damp walls, for about two weeks until they begin to shrivel and feel dry. They can then be used as required. Chillis preserved in this way are generally more pungent than the fresh variety.

Citrus peel is first pared from the fruit as thinly as possible, preferably in long strips, then threaded on to string and hung in a dry, airy place for about a week until completely dried out. Stored in an airtight container it should keep well for about 12 months.

Mushrooms are also easy to dry. Choose young specimens and thread them carefully on to string through the stem. Then hang to dry for several days, taking care they do not bunch together. During the summer most varieties of mushroom can be spread out on a tray and left in the sun until completely dried out. Before use, dried mushrooms must be reconstituted by soaking.

Among the simplest delicatessen-style meats to produce at home is the plain roast. Simply buy a joint from the butcher, roast it, leave to cool, slice and serve cold. A more elaborate alternative is the spiced beef described below. The pages that follow also include a varied selection of recipes for home-made sausages, without casing, which are both very tasty and easy to make. Very soon you will be wondering why you did not start making your own sausages years ago.

Remember that both garlic and chillis have natural preservative qualities and can be added to dishes where appropriate.

Spiced beef

This is a delicious dish for a festive occasion, especially a buffet.

SERVES 10

1 oz (25 g) black peppercorns
1 oz (25 g) allspice berries
1 oz (25 g) juniper berries
1 oz (25 g) molasses sugar

5 lb (2.5 kg) lean silverside, in one
  piece
¼ pint (150 ml) strong cider
  vinegar

Crush the spices roughly, mix with the sugar and rub into the meat. Place the meat in a bowl and leave in a cool place. Each day for the next week rub the spice mixture that falls off back into the meat. By the end of the week the meat will smell delicious.

Place in a heavy casserole and pour over the vinegar. Cook at 275°F/140°C/Gas 1 for 5 hours. Leave in the dish to cool for 3 hours. Remove from the dish. Wrap in foil and place under a heavy weight until the next day. Carve thinly and serve with bean salads.

Note The sugar in this recipe is not absolutely essential, but it does have some preservative qualities and also gives a piquant element to the flavour.

Potted herrings

These taste good served with wholemeal toast, or
as part of a mixed hors d'oeuvres.

SERVES 2

3 herrings, scaled, gutted and cleaned
1 bay leaf, crumbled
12 allspice berries, crushed

freshly ground black pepper
cider vinegar (quantity
  depending on container)

Chop the fish finely (do not use a food processor because this will produce ground fish). Place in the bottom of an earthenware casserole. Sprinkle with the bay leaf, allspice berries and pepper. Just cover with vinegar, then cover the dish with tinfoil. Place in a very low oven, at 275°F/140°C/Gas 1, for 8 hours or overnight. Remove and store in a cool pace. When cold, drain off any excess liquid and place a heavy weight on top of the fish in its casserole for another 5 hours.

The fish will keep for up to 10 days in the refrigerator.

Hummus

This is a classic Mediterranean-style vegetable pâté.

8oz (225g) chick peas
2 cloves garlic, crushed
1 onion (optional)

4oz (100g) tahini
lemon juice
olive oil

Soak the chick peas in plenty of water overnight. Rinse and cook in boiling water for at least 1 hour until well cooked through. Drain.

Liquidize the peas and add the garlic, onion (if using: it produces a more piquant dish) and tahini. At this stage the mixture will be extremely stiff. Add in enough olive oil and lemon juice alternately to produce a smooth emulsion (it can be a little thin because it will firm up once chilled in the refrigerator for a couple of hours).

Serve well chilled, ideally garnished with fresh coriander leaves, black pepper and paprika.

Sausages

MAKES ABOUT 12

8oz (225g) meat (e.g. beef, lamb,
pork, chicken)

other ingredients ad lib
(see method)

Grind the meat very finely (this usually means putting it through a mincer at least twice). Add egg, cereal (e.g. high-fibre bran or oatmeal), herbs, spices, onion or even another meat: half beef/half pork sausages taste good.

Flour your hands. Break off the desired amount of meat mix. Roll between the hands to obtain a sausage-shape and dry-fry; or place on a non-stick baking tray and cook in the oven at 350°F/180°C/Gas 4 for about 30 minutes; or grill.

To be completely traditional, serve with lots of smooth mashed potato.

Sausages, chorizo-style

MAKES ABOUT 24

2 fl oz (50 ml) red wine
2 cloves garlic, crushed
½ teaspoon (2.5 ml) ground nutmeg
½ teaspoon (2.5 ml) ground cloves
6 black peppercorns

2 tablespoons (30 ml) paprika
pinch cayenne
1 teaspoon (5 ml) marjoram
1 lb (450 g) pork
8 oz (225 g) beef

Boil the wine with the crushed garlic, spices and marjoram. Leave to cool. Mince the beef very finely and the pork a little more coarsely. Strain the wine marinade and pour over the meat. Leave overnight. Shape the mixture into sausages. Leave to dry off and dry-fry or bake as required.

Spiced pork sausages

MAKES 16

12 black peppercorns
12 allspice berries
12 juniper berries
1 tablespoon (15 ml) mace

2 cloves garlic, crushed
1 lb (450 g) lean pork, finely ground
1 tablespoon (15 ml), sage, rubbed
wholemeal flour

Gently crush the spices and mix well with the meat and sage. Divide into sixteen equal portions. Roll into sausage-shapes and coat in flour. Grill the sausages under a hot pre-heated grill until crisp and brown.

Serve hot or allow to cool, then use as cold sausage, sliced.

Hot sausage and potato salad

SERVES 4

4 potatoes, cut into bite-sized chunks
8 oz (225 g) cooked home-made pork
   sausage (see spiced pork sausage
   recipe above)
1 onion, chopped
2 oz (50 g) almonds

scant ½ teaspoon (2.5 ml) celery seeds
¼ pint (150 ml) natural low-fat
   yoghurt
freshly ground black pepper
lovage leaves, chopped
1 teaspoon (5 ml) cumin seeds

Scrub and boil the potatoes. Meanwhile, combine in a large mixing bowl the sausages, chopped onion, almonds, celery seeds and yoghurt. When the potatoes are cooled, drain and combine, while still hot, with the other ingredients in the bowl. Add the pepper and sprinkle with lovage and cumin seeds.

Pork sausages

This recipe makes a part-vegetable sausage that is higher in fibre and lower in fat than the regular variety.

MAKES ABOUT 20

8oz (225g) lean pork, finely ground until smooth

2oz (50g) split lentils, well cooked

1 clove garlic, crushed

1 onion, minced

1 tablespoon (15ml) marjoram

generous shake worcestershire sauce

1 tablespoon (15ml) ground coriander

1 tablespoon (15ml) soft wholemeal breadcrumbs

1 tablespoon (15ml) mustard powder

1 egg

Combine all the ingredients together and beat to a paste. With floured hands take a small amount of the mixture and mix into small, bite-sized cocktail-sausage shapes. Place on a non-stick baking tray and cook in the oven at 375°F/190°C/Gas 5 for 25 minutes until cooked.

Serve as titbits on cocktail sticks or allow to cool and reserve for later use in hot sausage and potato salad (see opposite).

The mixture also makes a good savoury stuffing, similar to forcemeat.

Spiced sausage casserole

SERVES 4

4oz (100g) red kidney beans, soaked

8oz (225g) lean beef, minced finely

8oz (225g) lean pork, minced finely

1 tablespoon (15ml) oregano

1 tablespoon (15ml) paprika

2 teaspoons (10ml) chilli seasoning

1 garlic clove, crushed

freshly ground black pepper

2 tablespoons (30ml) wholemeal flour

8oz (225g) white cabbage, shredded

1 green pepper, sliced

1 onion, chopped

½ pint (300ml) stock

¼ pint (150ml) red wine

1 tablespoon (15ml) tomato purée

Cook the beans in boiling water for about 1 hour. Drain. Combine the meats and work in the herbs and spices. With floured hands roll the mixture into small balls. Place on a baking sheet and cook in a hot oven, 400°F/200°C/Gas 6, for 15 minutes. Remove the sausages from the tray with a slotted spoon, to drain, and put to one side. In a casserole, layer the shredded cabbage, pepper, onion and beans with the sausage balls. Blend any leftover flour with the stock, wine, tomato purée and sausage juices. Bring to the boil in a separate pan. Pour over the casserole, cover and bake at 350°F/180°C/Gas 4 for about 1 hour.

Sausage soufflette

SERVES 4

8oz (225g) lean lamb, minced	1 tablespoon (15ml) worcestershire
1 onion, minced	sauce
2 cloves garlic, minced	1lb (450g) parsnips, diced
2oz (50g) oatmeal	½ teaspoon (2.5ml) grated nutmeg
pinch celery seeds	¼ pint (150ml) low-fat skimmed
freshly ground black pepper	milk
dash Tabasco sauce	2 eggs, separated
1 tablespoon (15ml) ground	1 tablespoon (15ml) sunflower
cumin	seeds, toasted
1 tablespoon (15ml) oregano	1oz (25g) low-fat Cheddar, grated

Combine the first ten ingredients and mix together well. Divide into six and form into sausage-shapes. Place in an ovenproof dish and bake in the oven at 400°F/200°C/Gas 6 for 15 minutes.

Meanwhile boil the parsnips until soft and drain. Beat well to make a smooth purée. Add in the milk and nutmeg. When smooth beat in the egg yolks. Whisk the egg whites and fold into the mixture. Remove the dish from the oven. Spoon the parsnip mixture over the top. Dot with the sunflower seeds and sprinkle on the cheese. Return to the oven for 30 minutes until risen and golden.

Carrot spread

If you are cutting down on sugar, salt and fats one of the problems is bread – what do you put on it? The following is a healthy, wholefood answer. Without the yoghurt, however, this makes a refreshing starter served with a garnish of orange and watercress.

½oz (15g) butter	2 tablespoons (30ml) natural low-
4oz (100g) carrots, scrubbed and	fat yoghurt (optional: omit for a
grated	thicker consistency)
1 small onion, grated	grated rind and juice of
4oz (100g) curd cheese	1 orange

Melt the butter in a non-stick pan. Add the carrot and onion and cook over a low heat until the onion is soft and transparent. When the vegetables are fully cooked mix together in a bowl with the cheese, yoghurt and orange juice and rind (use a food processor for speed; otherwise work in slowly using a fork). Press into a suitable shallow dish and chill until firm. Spread on wholemeal bread.

Crustless curried quiche

This is just the sort of thing you might buy from your delicatessen on a hot summer's day, but this version comes without any harmful additives.

SERVES 6

1 onion, chopped

2 oz (50 g) mushrooms

1 tablespoon (15 ml) butter

1 clove garlic, crushed

1 small courgette, cubed

1 very small green pepper, sliced

1 tablespoon (15 ml) garam masala

4 eggs

4 oz (100 g) cottage cheese

¼ pint (150 ml) natural low-fat
   yoghurt

8 oz (225 g) spinach or broccoli,
   cooked and drained

coriander leaves to garnish

Sauté the onion and mushrooms in the butter with garlic. Add the courgette, green pepper and garam masala. Whisk the eggs. Add the cheese, yoghurt and spinach. Place the sautéd vegetables in an oiled quiche dish and pour over the egg mixture.

Bake at 325°F/160°C/Gas 3 for 40 minutes or until the centre is firm.

Garnish with fresh coriander leaves.

CHAPTER FOUR

A pinch of salt

Salt is an essential component of the human body. It is also a mineral found occurring naturally in most fresh foods. However, it is also added to most prepared foods, for flavour, and the quantities in which it is added have for some years been giving cause for alarm. Salt has been implicated as a 'killer' substance causing disorders that vary from hypertension to arthritis, including anxiety, stress and pre-menstrual tension (PMT). Salt is addictive and, some have claimed, potentially lethal.

The chemical name of table salt is sodium chloride, comprising about 40 per cent sodium and 60 per cent chloride. A teaspoonful contains approximately 2.5 grams each of sodium and chloride, and it is the sodium element that is considered 'bad' for us because it causes water-retention: for every gram of salt consumed the body retains 70 grams of water. The kidneys retain water in order to dilute the sodium concentration, and it is this overloading of the kidneys that can lead to high blood pressure.

Although the most obvious source of sodium in the diet is that contained in table salt that we sprinkle on our food, there are of course many others. Processed foods contain it, and so does baking powder. Recent research suggests that a typical Western diet may contain as much as thirty times more sodium than the body requires.

Sodium and chlorides occur naturally in a wide range of foods, though the proportions vary: in lettuce, for example, they are low, in watercress medium, and in beetroot high. A salt deficiency is therefore unlikely to occur under any normal circumstances. A diet without salt or salt products added to it and comprising only moderate amounts of milk, meat, cheese and fish will still provide over 2 grams of sodium daily – five times greater than the body's minimum requirement.

Tests carried out by the Israeli army while on manoeuvres in the desert have shown that salt was not needed as a dietary replacement even in sweat-inducing conditions where the body loses salt. The soldiers on a no-added-sodium diet were able to perform just as efficiently as the rest of the squad; their sodium intake from natural dietary sources was more than adequate for their physiological and psychological requirements.

Sodium chloride is not the only form of salt. Another mineral, potassium chloride, is also a 'salt' and is found in the cells that form body tissue. The sodium is in the plasma surrounding those cells. Too much sodium can cause potassium deficiency: the ideal is a balance between potassium and sodium.

Overall, the average person would benefit his or her health by cutting salt intake by about 25 per cent, for the wealth of evidence against it by far outweighs the claims of some recent media reports that the move to outlaw salt has been misguided. While the popular press seemed to imply that we could all go back to dousing our food with salt, the evidence previously accumulated in the case against salt in conditions such as hypertension, stress, fluid retention and PMT is too great to be ignored.

How can you go about reducing your salt intake? First, by removing the salt cellar from the dining-table. Then, stop adding salt to food as you cook it. If you miss the savoury edge its flavour gives to food, use herbs and spices more liberally to take its place. If cutting salt out altogether, at a stroke, is too drastic for you, take it gradually. Cut down little by little, or try a low-sodium seasoning from a healthfood store (these tend to be based on herbs, sea vegetables and seeds, and some are entirely free of salt). If you find you must have salt, at least choose iodized sea-salt crystals.

Thirdly, try to avoid buying convenience foods – or, more particularly, processed foods. It is not only peanuts and potato crisps to which manufacturers add salt; canned soups and vegetables contain it – and so do cakes and desserts. Even some otherwise additive-free frozen foods contain salt. Before you buy manufactured foods, of any kind, look at the labels. It is possible to buy vegetables that have been canned without salt being added, and salt-free cheese and baked goods, including bread, are now on sale. Crispbread, tomato purée, spreading fats and other manufactured food items are also available in salt-free versions (that is, free of added salt). Failing salt-free, look for low-salt products. Bear in mind when shopping that salted butter contains 30 times as much sodium as unsalted, and that golden syrup contains 25 times as much sodium as honey.

Many different types of salt are used in food manufacture. The word 'sodium' is always a give-away. For example, sodium citrate and sodium bicarbonate are two common additives. Sodium benzoate is often mixed in salad dressings and chutneys. Other compounds include sodium sulphite, used to bleach fruit, and sodium ascorbate, used in the pharmaceutical industry and frequently contained in vitamins sold over the counter. Another form of sodium is monosodium glutamate (MSG). This is particularly hazardous because without actually tasting salty is has three times the sodium content of sodium chloride. Words such as disodium and soda (derived from 'sodium') also signify salt content; so do abbreviations such as 'bicarb', for bicarbonate of soda, and 'Na', the chemical symbol for sodium. 'Brine' is a salt solution. Finally, the adjectives 'kippered', 'smoked' and 'self-raising' also denote the presence of salt in some form. It is not an easy substance to avoid.

Sodium (salt) content per 4 oz (100 g) food

	mg sodium		mg sodium
FLOUR AND FLOUR PRODUCTS		VEGETABLES	
barley	5	globe artichoke	6
wholemeal bread	540	beans, fresh runner	2
wholemeal flour	3	mung beans	820
CEREALS		broccoli	6
muesli	180	carrots	25
DAIRY PRODUCTS		lentils	12
fresh whole milk	50	mushrooms	9
skimmed milk	52	watercress	60
goat's milk	40	FRUITS	
butter, salted	870	apples	2
butter, unsalted	7	NUTS	approx. 5
Edam	980	SWEETENEERS	
Cheddar	610	demerara sugar	6
cottage cheese	450	honey	11
natural yoghurt	76	golden syrup	275
eggs	140	MISCELLANEOUS MANUFACTURED	
OTHER FATS		FOODS	
low-fat spread	690	milk chocolate	120
margarine	800	instant coffee	4000
MEAT AND MEAT PRODUCTS		mayonnaise	360
bacon	approx. 2000	curry powder	450
beef, lean	61	baking powder	
chicken	81	(sodium bicarbonate)	11800
lamb, lean	88	beef extract	4800
pork, lean	70	vegetable extract	4500
salami	1859	table salt	38850
FISH		soy sauce	7340
cod fillet	77		
cod, smoked	1170		
herring	67		
kipper	990		
prawns	1590		

Note Crispbread, tomato purée, spreading fats and canned vegetables are among the foods now available in salt-free versions.

For most people a balanced diet of unrefined foods will ensure a reasonable, and certainly an adequate, salt intake. However, there are certain foods which, although 'natural', are high in sodium. If for medical reasons you need to adhere strictly to a low-sodium diet, you should avoid, or severely restrict, these foods. The rest of us would also do well to be aware which foods are high in sodium so that we can balance meals accordingly. The table opposite shows the sodium content of some common foods.

Cooking without salt

Perhaps the idea of not adding salt to vegetables when you cook them is anathema. But remember that you do not have to boil them in water, which leaches out flavour and nutrients alike. Try steaming or stir-frying them. Served straight from the steamer dressed with a little lemon juice, yoghurt or sesame seed 'salt', they are delicious.

Sesame seed salt, sometimes known as gamasio, is one of several sesame seed-based seasonings now widely available. It contains half as much sodium as regular table salt. To make your own, take several spoonfuls of sesame seeds, toast them in a dry non-stick frying-pan and when brown remove them from the heat and allow to cool. Grind finely in a food-processor or liquidizer – or by hand. Store in a screw-top jar.

Simply beans

This dish has a sodium content per serving of only 1 mg.

SERVES 2

*8oz (225g) green string beans,
    topped and tailed*
1 teaspoon (5ml) lemon juice
*1 teaspoon (5ml) natural low-fat
    yoghurt*

*1 teaspoon (5ml) home-made
    mayonnaise*
sesame seeds, powdered
*freshly ground black pepper
    (optional)*

Place the beans in a steamer for about 10 minutes. Remove while still bright green and crunchy. Mix the lemon juice, yoghurt and mayonnaise together well by shaking. Pour this dressing over the beans before serving. Sprinkle with crushed sesame seeds and, if liked, black pepper.

Orange baked potatoes

1lb (450g) sweet potatoes
(preferably a bright pink colour)
2 small satsuma-type oranges, or the
equivalent quantity of drained
canned mandarins in natural juice

oil
freshly ground black pepper
2 cardamon pods

Scrub the potatoes and cut into even-sized wedges. Do not peel. Cook in boiling water. Drain.

Peel the oranges, unless using canned. Heat a little oil in a non-stick frying-pan. Add the potatoes and brown well. Stir in the seasoning and juice. Heat through and add the orange segments. Mix.

Turn into a shallow ovenproof dish. Keep warm in the oven or re-heat later under the grill.

Green pâté

This makes a good first course served with wholemeal toast.

SERVES 4

8oz (225g) shelled broad beans
2oz (50g) fresh peas
4oz (100g) very lean unsmoked
bacon
1 small onion, chopped

2 tablespoons (30ml) natural low-
fat yoghurt
lemon juice
1 tablespoon (15ml) or more fresh parsley
2 hard-boiled eggs

Steam the beans until cooked. Mince the bacon. Blanch the peas. Sauté the bacon in a non-stick frying-pan until it is transparent. Place the onion, beans, bacon mixture and yoghurt in a liquidizer. Blend until smooth. Mix carefully with the peas, lemon juice, herbs and chopped egg. Press into a pâté dish and chill.

Bacon leaf salad

SERVES 2

4 rashers bacon, cut into small pieces
1 bunch spinach leaves, watercress
or cos lettuce heart

2oz (50g) hazelnuts
4 salad onions, snipped
freshly ground black pepper

Dry-fry the bacon until crisp in a non-stick frying-pan. Remove from the heat. Place the shredded green leaves in a salad bowl.

Add the hazelnuts to the bacon, heat through, then tip the contents of the pan over the leaves. Toss well. Garnish with the onions, season with black pepper and serve while still warm.

Skordalia sauce

This is a Greek-Cypriot dish.

2 cloves garlic, chopped
3 tablespoons (45 ml) chopped
   flat-leaved parsley
1 large potato, washed and boiled
2 oz (50 g) ground almonds

4 tablespoons (60 ml)
   red wine vinegar
4 fl oz (100 ml) olive oil
freshly ground black pepper

Combine the garlic, parsley, potato and almonds in a mixer. Add the vinegar. Continue mixing and add the olive oil, little by little, in a steady stream as for mayonnaise. (The amount of oil needed will depend on the size and texture of the potato.) The mixture should acquire the consistency of thick mayonnaise. Season with black pepper.

Serve with crunchy salads or kebabs and wholemeal pitta bread.

Sandwich spread

This is a good spread for a wholemeal sandwich filled with sprouted alfalfa beans, or with toast, or on rye crispbread. It is also suitable for canapés.

4 oz (125 g) red split lentils
7 fl oz (200 ml) water
2 oz (50 g) low-fat spread
2 tablespoons (30 ml) chopped
   flat-leaved parsley

1 onion, chopped
1 tablespoon (15 ml) lemon juice
1 pinch chilli seasoning
a good pinch cumin powder
freshly ground black pepper

Put the lentils in a saucepan with the water and cook until the liquid has been absorbed (about 25 minutes). Beat the low-fat spread into the lentils with the parsley, onions, lemon juice and seasoning. It should make a smooth, thick paste.

More lemon juice or a crushed garlic clove may be added to taste.

Spinach pudding

SERVES 4

2 oz (50 g) polyunsaturated
margarine
1 small onion, chopped
1 lb (450 g) cooked spinach, drained
and chopped
1 oz (50 g) wholemeal flour

1 teaspoon (5 ml) mustard powder
⅓ pint (220 ml) low-fat skimmed milk
1 oz (25 g) low-fat Cheddar, grated
3 eggs, separated
freshly ground black pepper
freshly grated nutmeg

Melt half the margarine and sauté the onion. Add the spinach and cook for about 5 minutes until the liquid has evaporated and the mixture is beginning to stick.

In a separate pan melt the rest of the margarine, add the flour, mustard and milk. Remove from the heat and beat in the cheese, spinach mixture, egg yolks and seasonings. Whisk the egg whites and fold into the mixture.

Pour the mixture into a well-oiled pudding-basin or ovenproof mould and cover the top with a sheet of greaseproof paper. Place in a water bath and bake at 350°F/180°C/Gas 4 or for about 1 hour until the centre is firm and springy to the touch.

Allow to stand for 5 minutes, then turn out on to a serving dish.

Serve with a home-made pasta sauce or a tomato sauce for a totally vegetarian dish.

Spinach nut ring

This dish is good as a vegetarian main course or used as a side dish.

SERVES 4 (MORE IF PART OF A BUFFET)

1 onion, finely chopped
1 tablespoon (15 ml) oil
1 small green pepper, chopped
2 stalks celery, chopped
1 lb (450 g) cooked spinach, well
drained and chopped
4 oz (100 g) nuts, chopped
4 oz (100 g) curd cheese
2 eggs, beaten with cheese

1 fl oz (25 ml) lemon juice
1 teaspoon (5 ml) grated nutmeg
8 oz (225 g) soft wholemeal
breadcrumbs
freshly ground black pepper
2 tablespoons (30 ml) wheatgerm, or
Parmesan cheese (which has a
higher saturated fat content)

Sauté the onion in the oil. Add the pepper and celery. Cook for 5 minutes. Add the spinach and mix well. Stir in all the remaining ingredients except the wheatgerm. Oil a ring mould, using a brush or kitchen-towel pad to ensure complete coverage (do not skimp on oil at this stage or the ring mould will break up when you try to unmould it).

Sprinkle the wheatgerm over the inside of the mould, covering evenly. Pour in the spinach mixture. Set the mould in a bath of water three-quarters full. Bake at 375°F/190°C/Gas 5 for 40 minutes or until set.

Turn out on to a plate to serve. Garnish with carrot slices around the edge and fill the centre with tomato salad.

Green rice bake

SERVES 3–4

1lb (450g) spinach
1 tablespoon (15ml)
  polyunsaturated margarine or
  butter
2 tablespoons (30ml) wholemeal flour
1 pint (600ml) low-fat milk

2 tablespoons (30ml) cider vinegar
2oz Provolone cheese, finely chopped
1 teaspoon (5ml) grated nutmeg
8oz (225g) brown rice, cooked
4oz (100g) wholemeal breadcrumbs
  and sesame seeds, mixed

Cook the spinach, drain well and chop. Melt the fat. Add the flour and milk to make a white sauce. Gently stir in the vinegar. If the sauce curdles, continue stirring over heat until it becomes smooth. Stir in the cheese and nutmeg. Grease a 2-pint casserole. Spread the rice on the bottom. Cover with a thin layer of sauce. Add the spinach. Pour over the rest of the sauce, poking holes through the solid ingredients so that some sauce penetrates vertically. Leave enough to provide a good topping.

Sprinkle the top with the breadcrumbs and seed mixture and bake at 350°F/180°C/Gas 4 for 20 minutes.

Vegetable scotch eggs

MAKES 6

1½ lb (700g) potatoes, scrubbed
low-fat skimmed milk
1 teaspoon (5ml) chopped
  chervil
freshly ground black pepper

sprinkling mustard powder
6oz (175g) low-fat Cheddar, grated
6 small eggs
4oz (100g) oatmeal, or wholemeal
  breadcrumbs

Boil the potatoes and mash with the minimum amount of milk to a smooth purée, gradually adding the herbs, pepper, mustard and cheese.

Hard-boil and shell the eggs. Coat in the potato mixture, then in the oatmeal or breadcrumbs. Brown in a lightly oiled non-stick frying-pan or bake in the oven at 375°F/190°C/Gas 5 for 20 minutes: they can be stood end-up in patty tins. Serve hot or cold.

Squashed puff

SERVES 2

8–12 oz (225–350 g) pumpkin or other
   squash with green rind and yellow
   flesh, cooked (preferably steamed)
2 tablespoons (30 ml) wholemeal
   flour

1 teaspoon (5 ml) garam masala
1-inch (2.5-cm) piece fresh ginger,
   minced
3 eggs, separated
2 oz (50 g) pecan nuts, chopped

Mash the vegetable flesh and blend with the flour, seasoning and egg yolks until smooth. Whisk the egg whites until double in volume. Fold into the squash mixture.

Turn into an oiled soufflé dish. Sprinkle the chopped nuts round the sides. Bake at 350°F/180°C/Gas 4 for 45 minutes or until puffed and golden. Serve straight away.

Courgette sambal

This Indonesian dish makes a refreshing salad accompaniment for European dishes, or can be served as part of an Eastern meal.

SERVES 2

2 courgettes, finely chopped
1 green pepper, chopped
2 tomatoes, chopped
4 spring onions, chopped
1 teaspoon (5 ml) cumin seeds

1½ tablespoons (20 ml) olive oil
3 tablespoons (45 ml) red wine vinegar
½ level teaspoon (2 ml) thyme
½ teaspoon (2.5 ml) tarragon
a few round lettuce leaves

Combine all the vegetables. Toast the seeds and slightly crush. Add to the oil, vinegar and herbs. Toss the vegetables in the dressing and arrange on a round bed of lettuce leaves.

If serving with other Eastern dishes, sprinkle a few toasted coconut flakes on top to give an authentic flavour.

Mint dressing

2 tablespoons (30 ml) orange juice
1 tablespoon (15 ml) olive oil
3 tablespoons (45 ml) lemon juice

1 tablespoon (15 ml) mint
freshly ground black pepper

Combine all the ingredients in a liquidizer. Chill.

Avocado ring

2 teaspoons (10ml) vegetable setting
  agent mixed with 2 tablespoons
  (30ml) cold water
2 teaspoons (10ml) lemon juice
1 teaspoon (5ml) raspberry vinegar
1 tablespoon (15ml) honey
4 teaspoons (20ml) olive oil
4floz (100ml) cottage cheese
4floz (100ml) natural low-fat
  yoghurt
2 tablespoons (30ml) home-made
  mayonnaise

1 large avocado
1 small red pepper (or a canned
  capsicum), diced
1 tablespoon (15ml) diced sweet
  pickle
2 tablespoons (30ml) pecan nuts,
  chopped
2 spring onions, chopped
1 orange, segmented
6 grapes, halved and pipped
2 tomatoes, cut into eighths
top half small bok choi, shredded

Dissolve the setting agent in the water. Liquidize the next seven ingredients. Peel the avocado and cut in quarters. Thinly slice one quarter and reserve for garnish. Dice the remainder. Stir the setting agent into the cottage cheese mixture and add the pepper, pickle, nuts and onion. Mix well and pour into an oiled ring mould. Chill in the refrigerator until firm.

Unmould before serving. Fill the centre with *bok choi* topped with the orange segments, grapes and tomatoes and garnish with avocado slices. A trickle of mint dressing over the top (see opposite) just before serving is delicious.

Carrot and leek stir-fry

1 carrot, washed
1 leek, washed and cleaned
1 red or green pepper

2 teaspoons (10ml) olive oil
1 tablespoon (15ml) sesame
  seeds

Cut the carrot into four lengthways, then across into three. Cut the leek into similar-sized pieces. Cube the pepper.

Heat the oil in a wok or frying-pan. Brown the sesame seeds. Add the vegetables and stir-fry until the leeks begin to look translucent. The carrots should still be very crunchy. Serve.

Tomato soup

1½ lb (700g) tomatoes, preferably
  fresh
1 onion, chopped
1 stalk celery, chopped
1 carrot, chopped
1 tablespoon (15ml) olive oil

1 handful fresh basil leaves and a
  few leaves for garnish, or 1½
  teaspoons (7.5ml) dried basil
  leaves
2 pints (1 litre) vegetable stock
freshly ground black pepper

Chop the tomatoes (if using a food processor leave the skins on; otherwise, or for a finer, smoother texture, roughly chop and then push through a sieve). Sauté the onion, celery and carrot in oil. Add the basil and tomatoes. Add the stock and cook for 30 minutes. Liquidize only if a smoother texture is desired. Season with black pepper. Serve this clear soup garnished with basil.

For a cream soup, add 1 teaspoon (5ml) arrowroot before adding the stock and replace half the stock with low-fat milk, and serve topped with a spoonful of yoghurt sprinkled with paprika.

Tomato tower

This is an unusual accompaniment for grilled meats or
can stand alone as a lunch dish.

SERVES 2–4

12oz (350g) tomatoes, chopped
good sprinkling basil
8oz (225g) self-raising wholemeal
  flour
1 tablespoon (15ml) mustard
  powder

4oz (100g) polyunsaturated
  margarine
4oz (100g) Edam, grated
2 eggs
4 tablespoons (60ml) low-fat milk
2 shakes Tabasco sauce

Oil a large pudding basin. Place the roughly chopped tomatoes in it and sprinkle over the basil. Combine the flour and mustard. Rub in the margarine. Add the cheese, eggs, milk and Tabasco and beat until a smooth batter results. Spoon over the tomatoes.

Cook in the oven at 375°F/190°C/Gas 5 for 1 hour or until the pudding is well risen and golden brown. Turn out on to a serving dish.

Vegetable burgers

These are very nutritious, high-fibre burgers, high in polyunsaturates and low in saturated fat. They can be served in a wholemeal bun and topped with tomato, cheese, relish and salad, as for any burger. Note, however, that the same recipe can be adapted to include meat (see below).

2 oz (50 g) sunflower seeds, chopped
2 oz (50 g) peanuts, chopped
4 oz (100 g) pink beans, e.g. pinto, rosea or borlotti, cooked and chopped
4 oz (100 g) mixed grain (including millet, plus barley, oats and/or wheat), cooked

1 onion, chopped
several dashes soy sauce
several dashes worcestershire sauce
wheatgerm or oatmeal
freshly ground black pepper
sesame seeds (optional)

Combine all the ingredients using as much wheatgerm as necessary to prevent the mixture being too wet. Form into burgers, coat in sesame seeds (if liked) and either bake in a hot oven, 400°F/200°C/Gas 6, or cook over medium heat in a non-stick pan.

For meat burgers, add 4 oz (100 g) minced raw lean beef and cook for at least 20 minutes.

Baba ghanoush

This starter, or buffet dish, is Arabic in origin.

1 large aubergine
1 large clove garlic
1 small onion
4 tablespoons (60 ml) olive oil

6 tablespoons (90 ml) lemon juice
3 tablespoons (45 ml) tahini
freshly ground black pepper
coriander leaves

Prick the aubergine all over and bake in a medium oven, 375°F/190°C/Gas 5, until completely cooked. Allow to cool. (It is a good idea to cook the aubergine when there is something else in the oven.)

Peel the outer skin from the aubergine and put the flesh into a liquidizer. Peel the garlic and onion and add those to the aubergine. Liquidize for a few seconds. Add the oil and lemon to the liquidizer and blend well. Add in the tahini and mix well until pale, creamy and smooth.

Turn into a serving dish, season with pepper, coriander leaves and chill. Serve with warm wholemeal pitta.

Savoury bread loaf

It is worth making one of these to keep in the refrigerator
as a standby, because it can be sliced when needed,
much as you would a meat loaf.

SERVES ABOUT 4

6 slices wholemeal bread, torn up
   into little pieces
2 oz (50 g) wheatgerm
2 oz (50 g) non-fat dry milk powder
   and thin natural low-fat yoghurt
   or buttermilk
sprinkling nutmeg, thyme and
   sage, to taste

1 teaspoon (5 ml) low-sodium yeast
   spread
2 eggs
1 tablespoon (15 ml) butter, melted
dash worcestershire sauce
½ teaspoon (2.5 ml) onion purée
freshly ground black pepper

Combine all the ingredients, using enough yoghurt or buttermilk to
produce a fairly wet mixture. Leave to stand until the liquid has been
absorbed, then stir in the butter. Form the mixture into a fat roll (like a
swiss roll) and wrap in greaseproof paper or a clean tea-towel. Secure the
ends. Lower into a steamer and cook for about 30 minutes until firm.
Remove from the steamer, drain and slice and serve.

Alternatively, serve cold. Leftovers make a good filling for pitta. Cold
slices can be re-heated in spicy home-made tomato or pasta sauce.
Mushroom gravy is good poured over while hot.

Serve with bright green vegetables, for both colour and nutritional
balance.

The seasonings for this loaf may be varied to taste.

Hot Indian salad

This recipe was given to me by an Indian woman who runs
a grocery in West Ealing where I buy a lot of my spices and pulses.
I suggest green cabbage rather than the original white.

SERVES 4

1 lb (450 g) cabbage (spring greens,
   brussels tops or Savoy)
1 green or red pepper
pinch fenugreek seeds
pinch mustard seeds
small pinch asafoetida
2 large carrots, cut into julienne strips

1 tablespoon (15 ml) mustard oil
1 teaspoon (5 ml) turmeric
pinch chilli seasoning
freshly ground black pepper
pinch sesame salt
1 firm tomato, chopped

Finely slice the greens and pepper. Fry the fenugreek and mustard seeds in oil until they pop. Add the asafoetida. Mix. Add in the carrots, greens and pepper. Add the other spices and the tomato. Stir-fry until just cooked.

Serve with chapatti or wholemeal pilaff.

Made up in smaller quantities, this makes a good filling for wholemeal pitta sandwiches.

Ratatouille croustade

SERVES 4

6 slices wholemeal bread	*1 carrot, chopped*
1 clove garlic, crushed	*1 stick celery, sliced*
3 eggs, beaten	*6 tomatoes, sliced*
4 tablespoons (60 ml) wheatgerm	*at least 1 tablespoon (15 ml) tomato*
oil	*powder*
1 onion, chopped	*several dashes Tabasco sauce*
1 green pepper, chopped	*freshly ground black pepper*
2 courgettes, sliced	*generous sprinkling oregano and basil*
1 small aubergine, chopped	*2 oz (50 g) low-fat Cheddar, grated*

Tear the bread into small pieces and combine in bowl with the garlic, eggs and wheatgerm. Press the mixture into the bottom of an oiled, large shallow oblong baking dish. Bake in the oven, 375°F/190°C/Gas 5 for about 10–15 minutes.

Meanwhile, in a lightly oiled non-stick pan, brown the onion and add the green pepper, courgettes, aubergine, carrot and celery. Cook until the vegetables begin to go limp and the juices run. Add the tomatoes, seasonings and herbs. Raise the heat and add in the tomato powder, increasing the quantity if the mixture is too wet.

Remove the crust from the oven. Pour in the vegetables and sprinkle over the cheese. Return to the oven for about 15 minutes.

To vary, add 2 oz (50 g) lean, minced lamb when the onion is browned.

Walnut potatoes

This rich supper dish can either stand on its own or be eaten with plainly grilled lean meat. Note that fresh walnuts contain 3 per cent vitamins. Per 4 oz (100 g), walnuts represent 525 calories, 10.6 g protein and 50 g fat.

SERVES 4

1 lb (450 g) potatoes
1 onion, chopped
pinch nutmeg
2 tablespoons (30 ml) chopped parsley
skimmed milk
3 eggs, separated

4 oz (100 g) mild cream cheese, e.g. Dolcelatte
4 oz (100 g) cottage or curd cheese
¼ pint (150 ml) natural low-fat yoghurt
3 oz (75 g) walnut halves
freshly ground black pepper
coriander leaves

Boil the potatoes and drain. Cream the potatoes together with onion, nutmeg, parsley and enough milk to make a creamy mash. Whisk the egg whites and fold into the mixture. Place in an oiled ovenproof dish. Mix the cheeses together until smooth, either by hand or in a food processor. Add the yoghurt and egg yolks. Beat well and pour over the potatoes.

Decorate with walnut halves. Bake at 350°F/180°C/Gas 4 for 30 minutes until the top is golden. Sprinkle with pepper and garnish with coriander leaves.

Golden berry bake

SERVES 4

1 pint (600 ml) water
8 oz (225 g) wheat berries
2 onions, chopped
2 cloves garlic, crushed
1 small head cauliflower, separated
    into florets

sprinkling soy sauce
2 eggs, whisked
¼ pint (150 ml) natural low-fat yoghurt
4 oz (100 g) low-fat cream cheese, e.g. curd or
    Bel Paese
3 tablespoons (45 ml) oatmeal

Bring the water and berries to boil in a saucepan and cook for 50 minutes until the berries are soft and the water absorbed. Lightly oil a non-stick pan and sauté the onion and garlic. Add the cauliflower and stir-fry until softened but still with some bite. Turn the cooked wheat into a round 2-pint casserole dish and stir in the soy sauce. Stir in half the eggs. Add the vegetables. Whisk the yoghurt into the remaining egg with the cheese. Add in the oatmeal. Pour over the casserole. Bake at 350°F/180°C/Gas 4 for 20 minutes until cooked and golden.

To vary, add 4 oz (100 g) cooked chicken or turkey pieces with the cauliflower.

CHAPTER FIVE

Sweet enough without it

Sugar occurs naturally in fruits, grains and vegetables. If the diet contains these in adequate proportions the body can metabolize carbohydrates to provide more than sufficient sugar for its energy needs. Over the last few decades, however, the Western world's consumption of complex carbo-hydrates has decreased while that of refined sugar has increased. Refined sugar provides only empty calories, and one startling fact to note is that most obese people, who probably consume a lot of sugar, are badly malnourished.

White sugar

Refined white sugar, or sucrose, causes obesity and dental caries as well as being implicated in many more serious diseases. It serves no useful nutritional purpose at all. Like salt, it is added to most manufactured convenience foods, not just the obviously sweet products such as instant desserts but canned vegetables and manufactured meat products, too. Meat products can contain as much as 3 per cent added sugar, processed vegetables as much as 13 per cent. Commercially produced ice cream, already indicted in this book for its saturated fat content and undesirable additives, is also high in sugar. Just cutting out manufactured foods from the diet would drastically reduce sugar intake.

According to Professor John Yudkin, the author of *Pure, White and Deadly*, high sugar intake may be the single most important factor in the production of artery-clogging blood fats. He argues that if only a fraction of what is already known about the effects of sugar were to be revealed in relation to any other material used as a food additive, 'that material would be promptly banned'.

All sugars and starches are converted by the digestive juices into a simple sugar called glucose, or blood sugar. Glucose is added to food as dextrose, grape sugar or even corn syrup. Any sugar, in whatever form, disturbs the calcium-phosphorus level of the body for anything up to 72 hours: that is a long time for calcium, which plays an imporant role in the function of the heart muscles, to be out of balance.

Sugar also alters the body's levels of potassium and magnesium, which can lead to excessive perspiration, irregular heart beat and muscle cramps.

Sucrose is absorbed into the bloodstream very quickly, giving fast, almost instant, energy highs followed by slower and longer energy lows. Other forms of sugar (fructose, maltose and complex carbohydrates) are absorbed much more slowly, providing sustained and satisfyingly increased energy levels for far longer periods. However, any kind of sugar, complex or otherwise, taken in too high a quantity can produce the same instant highs and long lows. As always, balance is the watchword.

Alternative sweeteners

Giving up all forms of sweetener would be extremely hard for anyone, no matter how much they might deny having a sweet tooth. Luckily such draconian measures are unnecessary. Although the overall aim should be moderation, or preferably meanness, in the use of sweeteners, some, the unrefined products, are undoubtedly better than others. However, simply replacing white granules with brown is not the answer to the sugar problem, even if the brown sugar were unrefined molasses sugar. Outlined below are some of the commonest alternatives to the 'pure, white and deadly' sugar that still, for most of us, is what first springs to mind when we think of sweetening agents.

Fructose, or fruit sugar, comes from fruit. None the less, half its content is glucose. Isolated fructose, sold in chemists and other specialized outlets, is twice as sweet as sucrose (white sugar), so far less is needed.

Brown sugar, which includes molasses sugar (also known as black Barbados or demerara molasses), muscovado (also sometimes called Barbados sugar) and demerara, is about 94 per cent sucrose (as opposed to 99 per cent for refined white) with traces of the vitamins, minerals and protein left behind by processing. Raw sugar is made by evaporating off the water from sugar cane juice and allowing it to become solid and granulated in the process. Though no sugar is 'good' for you, if you look for the words 'raw cane unrefined' when buying sugar, and also reference to the country of origin (Guyana, Mauritius or wherever), you will at least be choosing the least of the evils, and certainly you will for the most part be avoiding dyed white, totally refined sucrose.

The different types of brown sugar available each have distinct characteristics. Molasses sugar is rich, dark brown, raw sugar with a strong, treacly flavour; the individual grains retain a light coating of molasses. Muscovado (dark, sticky and soft) also contains some molasses. Light muscovado is cream-coloured and has less molasses content. Demerara, with light, dryish crystals, is still classed as unrefined raw cane sugar.

Honey is a combination of fructose, glucose and sucrose, but unlike sugar it is believed to have an alkalizing effect on the system. Honey also contains small amounts of pollen in cloudy unfiltered varieties, which provides not only proteins but vitamin A and some of the B-complex vitamins, enzymes and minerals such as phosphorus, potassium, calcium, sodium, sulphur, iron, magnesium and manganese. It also has antiseptic properties.

Molasses is little more than sucrose with extra matter left behind by the sugar-refining process. It can be used, in preference to the further-refined treacle, in recipes requiring a strong, dark sweetening agent.

Blackstrap molasses, with a much stronger taste than regular molasses, is the liquor left when sugar-cane juice has been boiled down and the now-crystallized sugar has been removed. This residue contains B vitamins, calcium, potassium and more absorbable iron than is contained by, for example, eggs. It is thought to be a remedy for anaemia and constipation.

Maple syrup is a naturally derived concentrated sweetener, rich in sodium, potassium, calcium and phosphorus.

Artificial sweeteners

Artificial sweeteners are false friends in the battle against sugar, because although they are low in calories and do not cause dental caries the substances used in their manufacture are largely harmful.

Saccharin, for example, is manufactured from sulfonizol, a substance also used in certain drugs which are known to start allergic and toxic reactions affecting skin, the heart and gastro-intestinal tract. Saccharin has been shown to cause cancer in laboratory animals. The American Association for the Advancement of Science recommends its banishment.

Sorbitol is another sugar substitute, used even within the health-food industry. This substance has been found to be responsible for diarrhoea and digestive troubles, though it has not yet been pronounced unsafe.

Other sugar substitutes are thought to have adverse affects on the nervous system, the muscles and the heart. Those commonly available include manitaol, xylitol, miraculin, thaumatin, monellin, dihydrochal-cones, glycyrrhizin, acesulfam-K, cyclamate (under threat of banishment as a carcinogen) and one, aspartame, which though heralded as a 'natural' sweetener is in fact a chemical synthesis of the naturally occurring aspartic acid and the synthetic compound methyl phenylalanine.

The recipes for puddings and cakes that follow obviously include sweet-eners, but much less of them than you would usually find, and often in unusual forms. Full use is made of the sweetness of fresh and dried fruits. Raw brown and golden granulated sugars are used minimally; where possible, fructose, honey and molasses are used instead.

Cherry custard cake

4 tablespoons (60ml) butter
3 tablespoons (45ml) honey
4oz (100g) wholemeal breadcrumbs
4oz (100g) hazelnuts, ground
½ teaspoon (2.5ml) ground
  cinnamon

1lb (450g) cherries
2 tablespoons (30ml) sweet white
  wine
3 eggs
½ pint (300ml) natural low-fat
  yoghurt

Melt the butter and 1 tablespoon (15ml) of the honey together and pour into the combined crumbs, nuts and spice. Mix together well. Press into a lightly oiled 10-inch (25-cm) spring-form cake-tin and chill for several hours.

In a non-stick pan gently cook the cherries in the wine until most of the wine has evaporated. Place in a colander to cool and remove the cherry stones. Beat the eggs until very pale and increased in volume. Add the yoghurt and the rest of the honey and beat until smooth. Add the cherries and pour the filling on to the crumb base.

Bake at 350°F/180°C/Gas 4 for 40 minutes or until set and slightly brown. Decorate with angelica. Ideally, serve while still warm.

Malt bread

This tastes positively sinful, yet conforms
to principles of healthy eating.

5oz (150g) malt extract
4oz (100g) molasses
1oz (25g) polyunsaturated
  margarine
12floz (350ml) water
2 teaspoons (10ml) dried yeast

14oz (400g) wholemeal flour
8oz (225g) sultanas
2oz (50g) chopped walnuts
GLAZE:
  1 tablespoon (15ml) each water,
    sugar and low-fat milk

Put the malt and molasses into a saucepan with the water and margarine. Heat until the margarine melts. Cool. While still warm sprinkle on the yeast and mix well. Combine the dry ingredients in a mixing bowl. Add the yeast mixture and mix well for about 8 minutes.

Pour into a large, well-oiled loaf-tin. Leave to prove. When well risen bake at 400°F/200°C/Gas 6 for 45 minutes. Mix the glaze ingredients in pan. Bring gently to the boil. Brush over the loaf and leave to cool.

A Greek-style salad consisting of cucumber, tomatoes, onion, peppers and olives topped with goat's or sheep's cheese makes a nutritious and tasty dish.

Cottage teabread

This moist teabread is much lower in fat than most.

8oz (250g) cottage cheese
3oz (75g) fructose
3 eggs, whisked
2oz (50g) walnuts, chopped
  (reserving some for
  decoration)

4oz (110g) dates, pitted and
  chopped
8oz (250g) self-raising wholemeal
  flour
2 teaspoons (30ml) ground
  cinnamon

Beat the cottage cheese with the sugar until creamy. Add the eggs and beat into the mixture. Add walnuts and dates. Fold in the flour and cinnamon. Spoon into an oiled 1-lb loaf-tin and press the reserved walnuts down the centre in a line.

Bake at 350°F/180°C/Gas 4 for 45 minutes until firm and golden. Turn on to a wire rack to cool.

New Mont Blanc

This adaptation of a traditionally rich dish is made healthier by the use of yoghurt and egg white instead of whipped cream.

SERVES 4

1 lb (450g) chestnuts
1 vanilla pod
¼ pint (150ml) natural low-fat
  yoghurt

1 tablespoon (15ml) lemon juice
1 tablespoon (15ml) soft raw brown
  sugar
1 egg white

Peel the chestnuts and place them in a saucepan of water with the vanilla pod. Bring to the boil and simmer for 30 minutes. Drain, remove the pod and peel off the chestnut skins. Liquidize the flesh into a purée. Stir in the yoghurt, lemon juice and sugar. Mix well.

Whisk the egg white until double in volume. Fold into the chestnut mixture. Carefully pile on to a serving dish. Cap the mountain with another spoonful of yoghurt to make 'snow'.

Serve with wholemeal biscuits or wafers.

Dishes of fresh fruit are an ideal way to finish off a meal – much better than traditional stodgy puddings.

Pear and yoghurt custard flan

SERVES 4–6

4 oz (100 g) wholemeal flour
3 oz (75 g) polyunsaturated
    margarine
3 oz (75 g) ground almonds
1 oz (25 g) raw brown sugar
1 teaspoon (5 ml) cinnamon
3 pears

1 tablespoon (15 ml) cold water
4 drops almond essence
2 tablespoons (30 ml) lemon juice
2 eggs
½ pint (300 ml) natural low-fat
    yoghurt

Place all the dry ingredients in a mixing bowl or food processor. Mix to form a soft dough. Roll out the pastry and line an 8-inch (20-cm) flan ring. Bake blind at 400°F/200°C/Gas 6 for 15 minutes. Remove the greaseproof paper and bake for a further 10 minutes. Peel, halve and core the pears. Place in a saucepan with 1 tablespoon (15 ml) water, the almond essence and the lemon juice. Cover and poach for 5 minutes. Remove and drain well. Beat the eggs with the yoghurt.

Spoon half the custard into the baked flan case and bake for 20 minutes at 350°F/180°C/Gas 4. Then arrange the pear halves, cut side down, on top of the custard. Spoon the remaining custard mixture over the top and bake for a further 10 minutes until the custard is just set.

Light rice puddings

SERVES 6

4 oz (100 g) brown rice
1 pint (600 ml) skimmed milk
1 oz (25 g) raw brown sugar
pinch nutmeg

2 tablespoons (30 ml) all-fruit
    orange preserve without added
    sugar
2 eggs, separated
1 oz (25 g) flaked almonds

Place the rice in a saucepan with the milk, sugar and nutmeg. Bring slowly to the boil. Cook for 30 minutes, covered. Uncover and cook for another 15 minutes until the rice is tender and the milk absorbed.

Lightly oil six ramekins (or similar). Beat the preserve and egg yolks into the rice mixture. Whisk the egg whites until stiff and fold into the mixture. Spoon into the dishes and scatter the nuts over the top. Bake at 370°F/190°C/Gas 5 for 15 minutes. Serve.

Date bars

4 oz (100 g) polyunsaturated
  margarine
4 tablespoons (60 ml) honey
8 oz (225 g) wholemeal flour

4 oz (100 g) oats
4 oz (100 g) mixed nuts, chopped
4 oz (100 g) pitted dates, chopped
2 fl oz (50 ml) orange juice

Cream together the margarine and honey. Beat in the flour and oats. When smooth, add the nuts and beat again. Press half the mixture into a slightly oiled, non-stick, shallow cake-tin.

In a saucepan cook the dates in the orange juice until all the liquid has been absorbed. Spread the dates evenly over the oat mixture in the cake-tin. Spread the remainder of the oat mixture over the date filling and smooth the surface. Bake at 350°F/160°C/Gas 3 for 30 minutes. Allow to cool in the tin. Turn out and cut into bars.

Seedy teabread

This is a good example of a high-fibre, low-fat sweet dish, high in polyunsaturates thanks not only to the margarine but also to the sunflower and sesame seeds. The dried fruit, which keeps the bread moist, and the wholemeal flour give the loaf a significant fibre content. The amount of sweetener used is minimal, because the dried fruit is naturally high in fruit sugars.

4 fl oz (100 ml) water
8 oz (225 g) mixed dried fruits, includ-
  ing tree fruits (e.g. dried apricots)
2 oz (50 g) fructose
juice and grated rind of 1 lemon
8 oz (225 g) wholemeal flour
1 teaspoon (5 ml) baking powder

4 oz (110 g) wheatgerm
2 eggs, beaten
2 oz (50 g) polyunsaturated
  margarine
2 level tablespoons (30 ml) honey
1 teaspoon (5 ml) vanilla essence
4 oz (100 g) sunflower seeds

Boil the water. Remove from the heat and add in the mixed, chopped dried fruit, fructose, lemon juice and rind. Allow to soak for at least 15 minutes. Combine the flour, baking powder and wheatgerm. Beat the eggs into the fruit mixture with the margarine, honey and vanilla. Add the dry ingredients and combine well. Add the seeds.

Turn the mixture into a medium-sized, lightly oiled, non-stick loaf-tin. Bake in the oven at 350°F/180°C/Gas 4 for 45 minutes until the loaf is firm to the touch. Leave to cool in the tin for about 10 minutes and then turn out on to a wire rack.

Caramelized fresh fruit

*1 orange and 1 banana per
person*

little butter

sprinkling lemon juice

2 cardamom pods per person

raw brown sugar

Peel and slice the orange into rounds. Peel the banana and slice in half. Place the fruit in a buttered ovenproof dish. Sprinkle with lemon juice. Crush the cardamom pods and sprinkle over the top.

Taking pinches of sugar between thumb and forefinger, sprinkle sparingly over the fruit. Bake at 400°F/200°C/Gas 6 for 10 minutes until the sugar has melted and become sticky.

Muesli chews

MAKES ABOUT 12

*4 oz (100 g) polyunsaturated
margarine*

2 tablespoons (30 ml) molasses

2 teaspoons (10 ml) raw brown sugar

*12 tablespoons (180 ml) home-made,
sugar-free muesli*

Melt the margarine, molasses and sugar in a saucepan. Add the muesli and stir well to mix. Pour the mixture into an oiled, shallow cake-tin. Smooth the surface. Leave in a refrigerator to set. Divide into bars and store in an airtight container.

Muesli cookies

MAKES ABOUT 12

4 oz (100 g) wholemeal flour

*2 oz (50 g) home-made, sugar-free
muesli*

2 oz (50 g) raw brown sugar

2 teaspoons (10 ml) baking powder

*4 oz (100 g) polyunsaturated
margarine, or butter*

*1 tablespoon (15 ml)
honey*

Mix all the dry ingredients together. Place the fat and honey in a saucepan and cook gently over a low heat until all the ingredients are melted. Do not allow the mixture to boil. Pour the contents of the saucepan into the dry ingredients and mix well. Using a spoon, place small rounds of the mixture, well spaced, on a lightly oiled non-stick baking tray.

Bake at 375°F/175°C/Gas 5 for 15 minutes. Allow the cookies to cool on the tray for a short while before transferring to a wire rack.

Malted oat fingers

MAKES 6

4 fl oz (100 ml) oil
3 tablespoons (45 ml) malt extract
2 oz (50 g) raw brown sugar

4 oz (100 g) oat flakes
2 tablespoons (30 ml) sesame seeds,
  roasted

Heat the oil in a saucepan. Add the malt extract together with the sugar and heat until melted. Add the remaining ingredients and mix well. Press into a lightly oiled, non-stick, shallow cake-tin. Smooth the surface. Bake in the oven at 350°F/180°C/Gas 4 for 30 minutes. Cool in the tin, then transfer to a wire rack. When cool, cut into fingers.

Banana nut bars

MAKES ABOUT 12

4 oz (100 g) polyunsaturated
  margarine
2 oz (50 g) raw brown sugar
1 tablespoon (15 ml) clear
  honey

2 eggs, whisked
4 oz (100 g) wholemeal flour
2 teaspoons (10 ml) baking powder
2 bananas, mashed
4 oz (100 g) walnuts, chopped

Cream the fat and sugar together until light and fluffy. Add the honey and beat again. Add the eggs carefully. Add the flour, baking powder and bananas. Spread the mixture in a shallow, lightly oiled non-stick cake-tin. Sprinkle the chopped walnuts on top.

Bake in the oven at 375°F/190°C/Gas 5 for 20 minutes until light, risen and springy to the touch. Leave to cool in the tin for a couple of minutes, then divide into bars and transfer to a wire rack to cool.

Muesli flapjacks

MAKES ABOUT 12

4 oz (100 g) polyunsaturated
  margarine
2 fl oz (50 ml) clear honey

2 oz (50 g) raw brown sugar
10 oz (275 g) home-made, sugar-free
  muesli

Melt the margarine, honey and sugar in a saucepan. Stir in the muesli. Mix well. Turn the mixture into a shallow non-stick, lightly oiled baking-tin. Bake at 350°F/180°C/Gas 4 for 25–30 minutes. Allow to cool in the tin and divide into fingers. Cool on a wire rack.

Passionate carrot cake

2 bananas
6 oz (175 g) polyunsaturated
  margarine
4 oz (100 g) soft raw brown
  sugar
3 eggs, whisked
10 oz (275 g) wholemeal flour

grated rind and juice of 1 lemon
4 oz (100 g) ground almonds
10 oz (275 g) carrots, scrubbed and
  grated
4 tablespoons (60 ml) kirsch
  (optional)
2 oz (50 g) walnuts

Mash the bananas in a bowl. Add the margarine and beat until creamy. Add the sugar and beat until smooth. Beat the eggs, a little at a time. Stir in the flour, lemon rind and ground almonds. Mix well. Add the carrots, lemon juice, kirsch, if used, and walnuts. The mixture should be a soft dropping consistency.

Turn into an oiled, non-stick 12-inch (30-cm) cake-tin. Bake at 350°F/180°C/Gas 4 for 1–1½ hours until the cake is golden in colour and firm to the touch. If necessary, cover for the last 30 minutes. Cool on a wire rack.

Summer pudding

A favourite dinner-party dessert, this time with no added sugar.

SERVES 6

10 slices wholemeal bread, without
  crusts
1½ lb (700 g) soft fruit, mixed (e.g.
  raspberries, strawberries,
  blackberries, blackcurrants)

2 eating apples, cored and thinly
  sliced
white grapes to decorate (optional)

Oil a 2-pint pudding basin. Line the base and sides with slices of bread, trimming to fit. To ensure there are no gaps, slightly overlap the slices. Press the bread well against the sides. Prepare the fruit and place in a saucepan with the apple slices. Heat gently until the fruit juices begin to run out. Remove from the heat.

Put half the fruit in the basin and cover with a slice of the bread. Add the remaining fruit and use the last slices of the bread to make a lid for the top of the basin. Use a saucer, or any dish that is smaller than the rim of the basin, to fit on top of the bread. Press down with a weight and leave in a cool larder overnight.

To turn out, run a smooth knife round the inside of the rim. Cover the bowl with a serving plate and invert, shaking slightly to release the pudding. Decorate with white grapes.

Serve with thick natural-set yoghurt whipped with 1 tablespoon (15 ml) amaretto and a pinch of ground cinnamon.

Fruit and nut griddle scones

MAKES ABOUT 18

1 teaspoon (5 ml) honey	*2 tablespoons (30 ml) oil*
2 teaspoons (10 ml) dried yeast	*2 oz (50 g) sultanas*
1 lb (450 g) wholemeal flour	*1 oz (25 g) chopped walnuts*
1 egg, beaten	*½ pint (300 ml) water*

Blend the honey with 1 teaspoon (5 ml) warmed water. Sprinkle on the yeast and leave until frothy (about 5 minutes). In a large mixing bowl beat the yeast mixture into the flour. Add the egg and oil. Add the fruit and nuts. Beat again, adding the water, a little at a time, until a good, pliable dough is formed.

Cover the dough and leave to prove until double in size. Knock back, then roll out on a floured board to a thickness of about ½ inch (1 cm). Using a medium-sized cutter, cut out and place the scones on an oiled griddle tray. Leave to prove (about 30 minutes). Cook over a gentle heat for about 6 minutes each side until well risen and golden brown.

Wholemeal sponge

This recipe totally belies the notion that baking with
wholemeal flour produces heavy, stodgy results. Not only is this
sponge high in fibre, but it is fat-free too.

3 large eggs	*3 oz (75 g) wholemeal flour mixed*
3 oz (75 g) golden granulated	*with ½ teaspoon (2.5 ml) baking*
sugar	*powder*

Whisk the eggs and sugar together well until the mixture is much increased in volume, pale yellow in colour and leaves a trail from the whisk. Gently fold in the flour and baking powder. Spoon the mixture into two 6-inch (15-cm) oiled sponge-tins. Bake at 375°F/190°C/Gas 5 for about 25 minutes or until the sponges are firm to the touch and well risen. Cool on a wire rack. Sandwich the sponges together with sugar-free preserve or home-made lemon curd mixed with a little yoghurt.

Whole shortbread

5 oz (150 g) wholemeal flour
1 oz (25 g) whole rice or semolina
  flour

2 oz (50 g) soft raw brown sugar
4 oz (100 g) polyunsaturated
  margarine

Mix the dry ingredients in a bowl. Add the margarine and mix to a firm dough. Do not add liquid. Roll out the dough to a thickness of about ¼ inch (½ cm) and cut into rounds. Place on an oiled baking sheet and prick carefully with a fork. Alternatively, flatten the dough into a shallow, oiled cake-tin and score the shortbread into wheel spokes. Bake at 350°F/180°C/Gas 4 for 20–25 minutes until golden. The shortbread will become crisp as it cools.

When in season, mix chopped fresh fruit (strawberries, for example) with a little fresh yoghurt and use to sandwich two shortbreads together.

Peanut cookies

This low-sugar recipe is relatively high in fibre.
Despite the small quantity of margarine the recipe still works
because of the oil content of the peanuts.

MAKES ABOUT 16

3 oz (75 g) roasted peanuts
1½ oz (40 g) polyunsaturated
  margarine
1 oz (25 g) raw brown sugar

3 drops vanilla essence
1 egg
3 oz (75 g) wholemeal flour

Either grind the peanuts in a food processor or chop finely by hand.

Add the margarine and blend until mixed. Add the sugar and blend. Add the vanilla essence and egg and mix.

Add the flour gradually and blend to form a dough. Break off pieces of dough about the size of a small walnut and roll between the fingers to form balls. Place on an unoiled baking tray. Using the back of a fork, flatten the balls into disks, making grid patterns on the biscuits.

Place in a pre-heated oven, 375°F/190°C/Gas 5, for 10 minutes.

Remove from the oven and leave to cool on the baking tray. Do not try to remove while still warm. Store in an airtight tin.

Blueberry muffins

MAKES 12

6 oz (175 g) wholemeal flour, or 4 oz
   (100 g) wholemeal flour and 2 oz
   (50 g) corn meal
1 teaspoon (5 ml) baking powder
1 tablespoon (15 ml) lemon or orange
   juice

2 tablespoons (30 ml) runny honey
1 tablespoon (15 ml) safflower oil
4 tablespoons (60 ml) low-fat,
   skimmed milk
1 large egg
4 oz (100 g) blueberries

Combine the flour or flour mixture and baking powder. Whisk the juice, honey, oil, milk and egg together. Beat the liquid into the flour. When mixed add the blueberries carefully.

Lightly oil some patty tins and fill to about two-thirds full with the mixture. Bake at 350°F/180°C/Gas 4 for 30–35 minutes. Cool slightly and turn out to cool on a wire rack.

Banana ice cream

This is the easiest possible way of making ice cream.

½ pint (300 ml) cream and natural
   low-fat yoghurt (proportions to taste)
2 bananas

a little honey
rum
fresh orange juice

Whip the cream and yoghurt together. (On your first attempt, use rather more cream than yoghurt. Graduate to all-yoghurt ice when you have mastered the technique.)

In another basin whisk the bananas with a very little honey to taste, some rum and a little fresh orange juice to make a smooth, runny consistency. Combine with the cream and put into a freezer container.

Place in the freezer, turned to its lowest temperature. Unless using an automatic ice-cream machine, take the mixture out after 1½ hours and beat it again to dissolve any ice crystals that may have formed.

Replace in the freezer for another 3 hours until set.

Fruit butter

Fruit butters, descendants of medieval sweetmeats, are moistureless jams, dark in colour and made without added sugar. They are excellent spread on wholemeal bread, crumpets, muffins or scones and make a good alternative to honey or sugar-filled jams at the breakfast-table.

Almost any fruit can be used for fruit butters, but a high proportion of apple is important so that there is enough pectin for the butter to solidify. Apple and pear butters are both delicious, and you can also make mixed-fruit butter using whatever fruit is available. For a glossy 'black' butter use a dark fruit such as blackcurrants.

1lb (450g) apples　　　　　　　　　　　　　*½-inch (1-cm) piece cinnamon*
1 clove

Wash and slice the apples, removing the stalks and cores. Do not peel. Put the apple into a heavy saucepan with just enough liquid (e.g. water, wine or cider) to cover. Add the spices and peel and bring to the boil. Simmer, stirring, until the apples are very soft. Take great care not to let them burn (a heat mat under the saucepan would help). Strain and sieve. Return to the heat and continue stirring and simmering until the apple mixture is thick and dryish.

Lower the heat and continue stirring and cooking until a spoon drawn across the surface leaves a trail. Spoon the fruit butter into a shallow dish. Cover with waxed paper and store in a cool place. Either leave for several weeks to develop a good flavour or, if preferred, use straight away.

Fruit sugar

Fruit sugar, a very good substitute sucrose, can be made from raisins or dates which have been dried and ground. Raisins and dates are not only the sweetest of the dried fruits but have a significant fibre content. Dried fruit sugar can be used to make fruit butter, by combining it with water and oil. This makes a good alternative to honey. It can also be used for a syrup which is both higher in fibre and lower in calories than ordinary syrups.

1lb (450g) raisins, without stalks or seeds, or 36 dates, pitted and sliced

Spread the fruit on a baking tray and put into the oven at 250°F/120°C/Gas ½ for 12–15 hours. By then the fruit should have dried out and be rock hard. Allow to cool. Put the fruit, a little at a time, into a liquidizer and blend until reduced to a powdery, sugar-like substance.

One tablespoon (15ml) fruit sugar represents 0.5g fibre and 40 calories. This can be used in place of table sugar, on cereals, or whatever. When using it in cooking reconstitute the fruit sugar slightly by adding it with the liquid ingredients.

Nutty nibbles

Although made without added sugar, these bars are very sweet; they also have a significant fibre content and taste delicious.

MAKES ABOUT 18

6oz (175g) sesame seeds
8oz (225g) sultanas, chopped
6floz (175ml) water

6oz (175g) crunchy peanut butter
½ teaspoon (2.5ml) almond essence
(optional)

Toast the sesame seeds by placing them in a hot oven for a few minutes until they have turned a good medium-brown colour. Place the seeds in a saucepan with the chopped sultanas and the water. Bring to the boil and boil for 3 minutes. Remove from the heat and add the peanut butter and almond essence. Bring the mixture back to the boil, then simmer until a sticky paste is formed. Spoon into a shallow, oblong, non-stick baking-tin. Place in the refrigerator for one hour until set.

While still in the tin divide into about 18 small squares.

Chocolate biscuit cake

This cake is extremely rich, and intended as a dessert for dinner parties rather than for every day. It would also serve to satisfy almost anyone's craving for chocolate: a little goes a long way. None the less, it is healthier than similar cakes because comparable recipes usually specify twice as much chocolate, as well as considerably larger quantities of sugar and fat.

8oz (225g) plain chocolate, broken
4oz (100g) butter, cubed
2 eggs
1oz (25g) soft raw brown sugar
12 glace cherries, quartered
2oz (50g) almonds, chopped

2oz (50g) dried peel, chopped
1 tablespoon (15ml) grated citrus
  zest
8oz (225g) wholemeal digestive
  biscuits or similar, crushed
3 tablespoons (45ml) Cointreau

Grease a medium-sized spring-form cake-tin. Line with greaseproof paper.

Put the chocolate pieces and butter into a heat-proof bowl over a pan of hot water. Heat gently, stirring, until melted. Allow to cool.

Beat the eggs until pale and very frothy. Beat the sugar. Slowly stir in the melted chocolate mixture, fruit, nuts, peel and zest. Add the crushed biscuits and mix. Stir in the Cointreau and turn the mixture into the prepared tin. Level the top and cover with cling-wrap. Chill for 8 hours.

Turn out from the tin and serve cut into wedges while still chilled.

To vary, try carob bars instead of chocolate.

Apricot mousse

SERVES 6

12 oz (350 g) dried apricots
8 fl oz (225 ml) fresh orange juice
5 fl oz (150 ml) natural low-fat yoghurt

3 egg whites
orange segments to
garnish

Soak the apricots in the juice overnight. Poach gently in the juice until cooked, topping up with water if necessary. Place the apricots in a liquidizer and mix with the yoghurt. Whisk the egg whites until stiff and fold into the fruit mixture. Spoon the mousse into six individual serving glasses and decorate with the orange segments. Serve chilled.

Curd cake

3 oz (75 g) butter
8 oz (225 g) wholemeal biscuits,
    crushed
3 eggs
8 oz (225 g) curd cheese

1 tablespoon (15 ml) honey
finely grated zest of 1 lemon
2 tablespoons (30 ml) sultanas, soaked
    in 1 tablespoon (15 ml) orange juice
pinch cinnamon

Melt the butter and stir in the crushed biscuits. Use the crumbs to line the bottom of a 12-inch (30-cm) spring-form cake-tin.

Beat the eggs together until very pale and frothy. Gently stir in the remaining ingredients; mix well. Pour the mixture on to the biscuit crumbs and bake at 425°F/220°C/Gas 7 for 10 minutes. Lower the heat to 350°F/180°C/Gas 4 and cook a further 20 minutes until set.

Allow to cool slightly before removing from the tin. Serve either warm or cold.

Sticky fig loaf

4 oz (100 g) wholegrain cereal (e.g.
    muesli)
2 tablespoons (30 ml) honey
4 oz (100 g) dried figs, chopped

2 tablespoons (30 ml) nut oil (e.g.
    almond)
½ pint (300 ml) buttermilk
4 oz (100 g) wholemeal self-raising flour

Combine the cereal, honey, figs, oil and buttermilk in a bowl. Leave to soak for at least 1 hour. Lightly oil a non-stick loaf-tin.

Stir the flour into the wet fig mixture. Mix well. Turn into the prepared loaf-tin and bake at 350°F/180°C/Gas 4 for 1¼ hours until the loaf is firm to the touch and well risen. Leave to cool in the tin, then turn out on to a wire rack.

The loaf should be wrapped when cool and left for at least 24 hours to become sticky. It will become stickier the longer it is left.

Yorkshire cheese tart

SERVES 6

5 oz (150 g) polyunsaturated
  margarine
7 oz (200 g) wholemeal flour
2–3 tablespoons (30–45 ml) cold
  water
8 oz (225 g) cottage cheese

¼ pint (150 ml) low-fat skimmed
  milk
1 egg
1 oz (25 g) low-fat spread
2 tablespoons (30 ml) raisins
rind of half a lemon, grated

Make the pastry by rubbing the margarine into the flour until the mixture resembles breadcrumbs. Mix in the water to make a firm pastry dough. Roll out and use to line an 8-inch (20-cm) flan-tin. Chill.

Prepare the filling by sieving the cottage cheese, and combining it with the milk and egg. Alternatively, blend all the ingredients in a liquidizer. Add in the low-fat spread, raisins and lemon rind. Tip the filling into the pastry case. Bake for 30 minutes at 375°F/190°C/Gas 5, when the pastry should be cooked and the filling just set.

Rhubarb fruit cake

This cake is delicious served cut into wedges and
topped with home-made fruit yoghurt.

4 oz (100 g) polyunsaturated spread
8 oz (225 g) self-raising wholemeal
  flour
2 oz (50 g) raw brown sugar
3 oz (75 g) dried fruit (e.g. raisins and
  dates)

8 oz (225 g) uncooked, chopped
  rhubarb
1 egg, beaten
¼ pint (150 ml) low-fat skimmed
  milk
sunflower seeds for topping

Rub the fat into the flour. Add the rest of the ingredients, except for the seeds, but reserve a little of the sugar. Beat well. Pour the mixture into a 10-inch (25-cm) oiled cake-tin. Sprinkle the seeds and remaining sugar over the top. Bake at 350°F/180°C/Gas 4 for 1½ hours.

Cardinals' hats

2 oz (50 g) brown short-grain rice
1 oz (25 g) soft raw brown sugar
½ teaspoon (2.5 ml) ground
  cinnamon
1 pint (600 ml) low-fat skimmed milk
½ oz (15 g) vegetable setting agent

1 teaspoon (5 ml) vanilla essence
5 fl oz (150 ml) natural low-fat
  yoghurt
8 oz (225 g) raspberries
2 oz (50 g) flaked almonds,
  toasted

Put the rice, sugar, cinnamon and milk in a pan and bring to the boil. Simmer for 40 minutes or until all the liquid has been absorbed and the rice is soft. Melt the setting agent in 3 tablespoons (45 ml) water over a low heat.

When the rice is cooked beat in the vanilla essence until smooth. Add 2 tablespoons (30 ml) of the setting agent and beat well. When the rice has cooled beat in the yoghurt. Beat the mixture until smooth. Place the rice in four individual serving dishes and leave to set.

Thin the remaining setting agent with 1 tablespoon (15 ml) water. When dissolved, stir into the raspberries to glaze the fruit. Spoon the raspberries on to the rice and decorate with toasted almonds. Chill until ready to serve.

Plum pot

1 lb (450 g) plums
¼ pint (150 ml) red wine
2 tablespoons (30 ml) brandy
  or rum
stick cinnamon

juice of 1 lemon
1 tablespoon (15 ml) soft raw brown
  sugar
juice 1 small orange
almonds for garnish

Halve and stone the plums. Place in the bottom of a flame-proof dish.

In a saucepan bring all the other ingredients, including the plum stones, to the boil. Strain out the stones and pour the wine mixture over the plums. Leave to marinate for at least 4 hours. Before serving simmer on top of the stove, or cook in a medium oven, 350°F/180°C/Gas 4, for 20 minutes. Serve garnished with almonds.

Any leftovers can be stored in the refrigerator and served garnished with peeled orange slices.

Ricotta dolce

This is an authentic Italian dessert, rather like a hot cheesecake, but much lower in fat than most. It is ideal for dinner parties.

SERVES 6

1 lb (450g) low-fat ricotta
1 tablespoon (15ml) wholemeal flour
2½ tablespoons (40ml) honey
2 eggs, separated
½ teaspoon (2.5ml) saffron

2 teaspoons (10ml) grated orange peel
2 oz (50g) sultanas
1 oz (25g) dried mixed peel
½ teaspoon (2.5ml) ground cinnamon

Oil a loose-bottomed spring-form cake-tin. Beat together the ricotta, flour, honey, egg yolks, saffron and orange peel. Mix in the dried fruit. Whisk the egg whites until stiff and fold carefully into the mixture. Turn into the prepared tin and bake at 375°F/190°C/Gas 5 for 40 minutes until set. Remove from the oven and allow to cool. To serve, turn out on to a serving dish and sprinkle with cinnamon.

Mango mousse

SERVES 4

1 tablespoon (15ml) orange juice
1 tablespoon (15ml) lemon juice
2 tablespoons (30ml) white wine
½ oz (15g) vegetable setting agent
2 mangos, about 8oz (225g)

1 level tablespoon (scant 15ml) soft brown sugar
10 fl oz (300ml) natural low-fat yoghurt
2 egg whites

Mix together the orange juice, lemon juice and white wine and carefully combine with the setting agent.

Peel and slice the mangos and liquidize with the sugar.

Gently heat the setting agent mixture in a bowl over a saucepan of water until the powder is dissolved. Remove from the heat and stir in the mango purée. Leave until the mixture begins to set.

Beat the yoghurt, then beat in the mango mixture. Whisk the egg whites until stiff and fold into the purée.

Turn the mousse into a 1-pint charlotte mould and leave to set in the refrigerator overnight. Turn out to serve.

This recipe is suitable for most other fruits as long as the fruit juice used is of a complementary flavour.

Lime and melon mousse

This soft, light mousse is very refreshing after a rich main course.

½ ripe melon
large pinch ground ginger
2 tablespoons (30ml) home-made
  thick yoghurt
2 limes

2 eggs, separated
2 tablespoons (30ml) honey
½ oz (15g) vegetable setting
  agent
1 kiwi fruit, sliced, to garnish

Peel and de-seed the melon. Liquidize the flesh. Add the ginger. Beat the yoghurt and add to the melon. Peel the zest from one lime and add to the melon with the juice of the same lime. Reserve the other. Whisk the egg yolks until pale. Whisk in the honey.

Place the bowl over a pan of hot water and continue whisking until the whisk leaves an impression in the mixture. Remove from the heat. Pour the melon purée into the egg mixture, blending well. Dissolve the vegetable setting agent in 3 tablespoons (45ml) hot water, add a spoonful of the melon mixture and blend well. Pour the setting agent back into the melon purée, stirring all the time. Leave in a cool place for about an hour.

Whisk the egg whites until stiff and fold into the melon mixture.

Pour the mousse into an attractive serving bowl and place in the bottom of the refrigerator for 2 hours until set. Garnish with lime and kiwi fruit slices round the side of the dish and serve.

This mousse is best served scooped out with a spoon.

Fruit creams

SERVES 4–6

8oz (225g) dried peaches, soaked
  overnight in pineapple juice
3 bananas

5fl oz (150ml) natural low-fat
  yoghurt
toasted coconut flakes to decorate

Drain the peaches. Purée all the fruits together. Whisk the yoghurt and beat into the creamed fruit. Turn into serving dishes. Decorate with coconut and chill.

Whether cooked or raw, vegetables can be made more appetizing by dressing with home-made mayonnaise, yoghurt or a flavourful oil-and-vinegar dressing. Asparagus, avocodo, beansprouts and coriander are just some of the more unusual ingredients that can make a healthy diet an exciting one.

Fruit almond cake

8 oz (225 g) dried cherries or apricots
4 oz (100 g) polyunsaturated
  margarine
3 tablespoons (45 ml) honey
3 eggs, beaten

8 oz (225 g) self-raising wholemeal
  flour
4 oz (100 g) ground almonds
6 tablespoons (90 ml) sherry or
  amaretto

Cut the cherries in half, or quarter the apricots. Beat the margarine, add the honey and beat well. Gradually add in the eggs, beating well. Fold in the flour, fruit and nuts. Stir in the sherry. If the mixture is a little dry add a few more spoonfuls of sherry, to achieve a soft, dropping consistency.

Put the mixture into a large, oiled cake-tin and bake at 350°F/180°C/Gas 4 for 1½ hours until cooked in the centre (when a skewer pushed into the centre will come out clean).

Leave the cake to cool in the tin for 10 minutes, then turn out on to a wire rack.

Peaches with amaretto

SERVES 4

4 large ripe peaches
1 egg yolk
1 teaspoon (5 ml) honey

4 amaretti
1 tablespoon (15 ml)
  amaretto

Halve the peaches. Scoop out and reserve a little of the flesh to enlarge the cavity. Beat the egg yolk until pale and frothy. Beat in the honey. Crumble the amaretti and mix with the peach flesh. Add about half the liqueur and mix thoroughly. Pile the mixture into the cavities and bake in the oven at 375°F/190°C/Gas 5 for 20 minutes.

Serve with the remainder of the amaretto poured over and, if liked, flamed.

Ratatouille is a good example of a colourful and healthful vegetable combination.

CHAPTER SIX

Not a drop to drink?

Overhauling and re-thinking the diet along healthy principles must necessarily include an appraisal of liquid intake: not just the alcoholic element, but the other drinks which form such an important part of our daily routine.

Used sensibly, alcohol is known to have healthful benefits, such as reducing susceptibility to heart attacks. It also appears that alcohol may contribute to lowering cholesterol, although the recommended therapeutic 'dosage' is minimal (say, one glass of wine, or one single shot of spirits, per day), representing 4 per cent of the total energy requirement.

For most people a reduction in liquor consumption would do little other than improve general health. If you want to de-toxify your system totally and give up alcohol for a while you might wish to try the 'fake' cocktails and fruit 'wine' cups based on grape juice now on sale.

What of the other, non-alcoholic, drinks we rely upon so heavily?

Hard as it may be to believe, tea and coffee are not entirely harmless. Both contain caffeine, which is considered to be a major factor in high blood pressure. It causes agitation and irritation of the nervous system and is even believed by some researchers to be a carcinogen. The effect of caffeine on the central nervous system is to cause increased mental activity and heightened sensual perception. It is a controlling influence on the heart and kidneys, raising the pulse and stimulating diuretic activity.

Tea is lower in caffeine than coffee and Chinese naturally dried teas are a natural pick-me-up. If other stimulants containing caffeine are removed from the diet, weak tea could possibly replace them. Some of the more specialized kinds, such as souchong, green tea, jasmine, oolong or even kukicha are worth trying. The latter, sometimes called twig tea or *bancha*, is not strictly a tea because it is made from the twigs of the plant rather than the leaves, is very low in both caffeine and tannin and acts as an adaptogen, neutralizing acidic or alkaline conditions of the stomach.

If you have been a tea- or coffee-drinker all your life, finding palatable substitutes for these beverages can be very difficult. However, health-food stores sell many coffee substitutes, made, for example, from chicory and dandelion. Decaffeinated coffee beans and instant coffee are also available: these too can help with drink substitution. There are also a great many herbal tea combinations on the market that are really delicious if you can accept them on their own terms rather than expecting them to taste like Indian tea. Some of these are more than just substitutes and have been designed to do some positive good. Made from herbs, these teas (tisanes) have different effects ranging from calming (camomile) through invigorating (ginseng) to digestive (peppermint).

Finding other drinks to include in your regime may initially cause problems. Bottled mineral water has positive therapeutic benefits and almost medicinal attributes. It contains many beneficial minerals and its calorie rating is nil. Naturally sparkling mineral water is absolutely splendid in terms of health and refreshment but could become boring as an exclusive drink. All other bottled and canned drinks are bad news, even the low-calorie ones. What they have lost in sugar they have probably made up for with chemical additives and synthetic flavourings.

Although quite high in salt, canned mixed vegetable juices, available in various flavours including carrot and celery, are an excellent base for savoury drinks. They are ideal for a mid-morning pick-me-up, and their vegetable content gives them a fibre content of their own. Each 330 ml serving (one 11½ fl oz can) contains about one gram of fibre and approximately 66 kilocalories. Although very tasty on their own both their fibre and their vitamin content can be improved by mixing them with other ingredients.

The recipes in this chapter show how to make your own sweet drinks, with fresh fruits, and savoury ones, with vegetables.

Breakfast drink

This drink is really a meal in a glass, and by varying the
ingredients a different version can be made each time.
Starting with a banana, liquidize the fruit of your choice
with one, two or all of the following items:

natural low-fat yoghurt	*apricots*
orange juice	*wheatgerm*
apple juice	*sunflower seeds*

Chill. (Quantities will depend on what you have available: banana, yoghurt, orange juice and wheatgerm, for example, constitutes a complete meal in itself; banana and apple juice would make a breakfast drink to accompany other foods.)

Pineapple jogger

SERVES 4

12 oz (350 g) pineapple (fresh, or canned in its own juice)

¾ pint (450 ml) natural low-fat yoghurt

few drops grenadine (optional)

Blend the pineapple in a liquidizer. Add the grenadine and yoghurt. Blend until smooth and frothy. Serve in tall glasses, chilled.

Wheat and grapefruit drink

SERVES 2

2 large grapefruit

3 tablespoons (45 ml) wheatgerm

2 tablespoons (30 ml) honey

½ pint (300 ml) skimmed milk

Peel the grapefruit, remove the pith and pips and liquidize the flesh and juice. Add the wheatgerm. Blend in the milk until smooth. Chill and serve topped with yoghurt ice cream (see page 89).

Tomato tasty

SERVES 4

1 lb (450 g) tomatoes

1 small carrot, diced

1 stick celery, chopped

worcestershire sauce

dill weed

freshly ground black pepper

Blend the vegetables in a liquidizer. Add the worcestershire sauce, dill and pepper to taste. Serve chilled.

Kir cup

SERVES 4

4 oz (100 g) blackcurrants

½ pint (300 ml) white wine

½ pint (300 ml) sparkling mineral water

Blend all the ingredients together in a liquidizer and serve in wine glasses, well chilled.

Raspberry egg flip

SERVES 4

2 large eggs

1 tablespoon (15 ml) honey

4 oz (100 g) fresh raspberries

¾ pint (450 ml) sparkling mineral water

Separate the eggs. Whisk the whites until stiff. Beat the yolks with the honey until thick and creamy. Reserve a few raspberries for decoration and blend the remainder with the egg yolk mixture. Fold in the egg whites. Gradually add in the mineral water. Pour into tall glasses and serve decorated with a fresh raspberry.

Orange surprise

SERVES 2

½ pint orange juice

2 tablespoons (30 ml) lime juice

4 dried apricots

Blend all the ingredients together in a liquidizer and serve in wine glasses.

Honey yoghurt flip

SERVES 4

1 orange

½ pint (300 ml) sparkling
  mineral water

¼ pint (150 ml) thick-set yoghurt

2 tablespoons (30 ml) strongly
  flavoured honey

Liquidize the orange flesh and blend in the other ingredients. Serve in large glasses.

Adam and Eve

SERVES 4

2 eating apples, cored but not peeled

1 pear, cored but not peeled

½ pint (300 ml) sparkling
  mineral water

ground cinnamon

Liquidize the apples and pear together. Blend in the water. Serve well chilled with a sprinkling of cinnamon on each serving.

Cacik

SERVES 4

½ cucumber
½ pint (300 ml) natural low-fat
  yoghurt
small clove garlic, peeled

pinch mint plus fresh mint leaves for
  garnish
½ pint (300 ml) sparkling
  mineral water
cumin seeds (optional)

Blend the cucumber with the garlic and add the yoghurt. Add the mint and water and blend until smooth.

Serve in chilled glasses garnished with mint leaves, and, if desired, a few cumin seeds sprinkled on top.

Surprise iced tea

1 teaspoon (5 ml) honey
½ pint (300 ml) weak tea
2 tablespoons (30 ml) ginger wine

lemon slices
borage sprigs

Whisk the honey into the tea. Add the wine. Chill. Serve in wine glasses garnished with lemon slices and borage sprigs.

Ginseng pick-me-up

SERVES 6

½ pint (300 ml) ginseng tea
½ pint (300 ml) orange juice
2 tablespoons (30 ml) maple syrup

¼ pint (150 ml) sparkling mineral water
a little apple juice concentrate

Mix all the ingredients together and serve chilled in glass cups.

Strawberry shake

SERVES 4

½ pint (300 ml) natural low-fat yoghurt
8 oz (225 g) strawberries, prepared

2 oz (50 g) raisins
mint leaves for decoration

Blend all the ingredients together and serve chilled. Garnish with mint leaves.

Sparkling orange and blackcurrant

¼ pint (150ml) orange juice
¼ pint (150ml) sparkling
  mineral water

4oz (100g) blackcurrants
honey to taste
lemon slices

Whisk together the orange juice and water. Liquidize the fruit and add to the juice. Stir in the honey, to taste, and serve chilled, garnished with lemon slices.

Peach dream

4 large peaches, stoned and peeled
½ pint (300ml) natural low-fat
  yoghurt

½ pint (300ml) weak
  jasmine tea
cherries to garnish

Blend the peach flesh with the yoghurt and tea until smooth. Serve chilled in glass cups garnished with cherries.

Posset

3 egg yolks
¼ pint (150ml) white wine

1 tablespoon (15ml) honey
grated rind of 1 orange

Put all the ingredients into a double-boiler and whisk over heat until thick and frothy. Pour into heatproof glasses and serve immediately.

Fruit cooler

8oz (225g) lychees
¼ pint (150ml) natural low-fat yoghurt

2 tablespoons (30ml) strawberry syrup

Blend all the ingredients together well until frothy. Serve well chilled, garnished with fresh strawberries in season.

Summer punch

SERVES 6

1 pint (600 ml) herbal tea
2 tablespoons (30 ml) honey
¼ pint (150 ml) dark rum
½ pint (300 ml) white wine

½ (300 ml) sparkling mineral
water
1 small pineapple, peeled and diced
orange slices

Combine the tea, honey, rum, wine and mineral water and whisk well.
Turn into a large serving bowl and chill. Serve with the diced pineapple
and orange slices in punch glasses.

Caribbean cup

SERVES 4

2 passion fruit, without stalks
¼ pint (150 ml) apricot and orange juice

½ pint (300 ml) natural
low-fat yoghurt

Blend all the ingredients well. Sieve to remove the pips of the passion
fruit. Chill and serve.

Vitamin drink

MAKES 2 GLASSES

1 11½ fl oz (330 ml) can mixed
vegetable juice
1 tablespoon (15 ml) oatmeal

1 green pepper, de-seeded and
roughly chopped

Place the ingredients in a liquidizer and blend for about 1 minute. Chill.

Amber

SERVES 6

¼ pint (150 ml) apple juice
¼ pint (150 ml) pineapple juice
¼ pint (150 ml) orange juice

2 tablespoons (30 ml) fresh lime juice
½ teaspoon (2.5 ml) ground ginger

Whisk all ingredients together until frothy. Top up with mineral water if
liked and serve chilled.

Bitter lemons

MAKES 1½ PINTS (900 ML)

4 lemons   *honey to taste*
1½ pints (900 ml) sparkling mineral water

Cut the lemons into pieces and simmer in a saucepan with half the water for 15 minutes, with honey if using. Allow to cool. Strain. Top up with the mineral water and serve.

Orangeade

MAKES 1½ PINTS (900 ML)

4 oranges   *1 lemon*
1½ pints (900 ml) sparkling mineral water   *honey to taste*

Peel the rind from the orange carefully. Place in a bowl. Bring the water to the boil and pour over the rind. Steep until cold. Squeeze the juice from the oranges and lemon. Strain the water. Add the juice and a little honey if desired. Serve chilled.

Fruit squash

MAKES 1½ PINTS (900 ML)

4 oranges   *honey to taste*
2 grapefruit   *½ teaspoon (2.5 ml) vitamin C*
1½ pints (900 ml) sparkling mineral water   *powder*

Pare the rind from the fruit and place in a bowl. Bring the water to the boil with the honey and vitamin C powder. When dissolved, pour the liquid over the rind. Leave overnight.

Liquidize the peeled fruit and strain. Strain the liquid from the rind. Add the water to the juice and mix thoroughly. Dilute with more mineral water if desired.

CHAPTER SEVEN

Meals and menus

So that you can think in terms of combining dishes as well as ingredients in your 'new food' repertoire, this chapter shows what goes with what. For example, in a totally vegetarian meal a little more thought has to go into balancing proteins.

The advice that follows covers all everyday meal occasions, including breakfasts, vegetarian festive meals and barbecues.

Breakfasts

One of the following items, accompanied by fresh fruit and, perhaps, a herbal tea (tisane), will give you a healthy start to the day.

Muesli, moistened with skimmed milk, fruit juice or yoghurt

Wholemeal croissant with honey

Wholemeal muffins with 2 oz (50 g) low-fat cottage cheese

Wholemeal crumpets with fruit butter

Oatmeal mixed with fresh fruit

Wholemeal waffles and maple syrup

Egg on toast (to vary, mash hard-boiled egg with 1 oz/25 g low-fat curd cheese and a little low-fat spread with a fork until smooth and spread on wholemeal toast: this makes a little egg go a very long way)

Brunch

For lazy Sunday mornings when it is too late for breakfast and too early for lunch, brunch can take the place of both, and these dishes can be made in advance.

Home-made sausages

Kedgeree

Potato dosas

Grainy cottage cheese slice

Crunchy peanut bread and carrot spread

Corn crêpes
Malt bread
Tomato tasty
Pineapple jogger
Amber

Lunch

A balanced diet should include raw vegetables every day. Lunch is often the best opportunity. The simplest way to serve them is as crudités – a tub or dish of raw vegetables cut into finger lengths with an accompanying pot of well-flavoured dip. The suggestions below are for more elaborate meals, and could be accompanied by one of the fruit-based drinks suggested in Chapter 6.

Macaroni and wheat berry salad

Spinach eastern eggs, with a salad of raw cauliflower florets in dill/yoghurt dressing

Egg baked potatoes, served with a watercress salad with mint dressing

Neopolitan macaroni, with 'simply beans' (see page 89)

Egg patties, served on a platter of raw root vegetable fingers tossed in salad dressing

Bean loaf, served with a green leaf salad

Millet pilaff, with courgette chunks in a light curry-flavoured yoghurt dressing

Lentil slice, with coleslaw in yoghurt

Noodle eggah, with tomato and onion salad with basil dressing

Pizza (highly transportable and ideal for picnics)

Browned spaghetti toss, with raw fennel salad in yoghurt-based dressing

Fish koftas, with hot Indian salad

Green pâté, with chunks of wholemeal bread

Vegetable scotch eggs, with cold ratatouille

Vegetable burger, served in wholemeal rolls with mixed salad

Savoury bread loaf, with coleslaw in tomato yoghurt dressing

Ratatouille croustade, with mushroom tossed in dill dressing

Afternoon tea

Although not a meal occasion which finds much favour nowadays, particularly among the weight-conscious, it is always good to be able to indulge guests by offering something home-made when the opportunity for a real tea arises. Needless to say, any of the following suggestions are as good with morning coffee (or coffee substitute) as they would be with afternoon tea or tisane.

Malt bread	Fruit and nut griddle scones
Cottage teabread	Wholemeal sponge
Date bars	Whole shortbread
Seedy teabread	Peanut cookies
Muesli chews	Blueberry muffins
Muesli cookies	Ultimate cheese scones
Malted oat fingers	Nutty nibbles
Banana nut bars	Sticky fig loaf
Muesli flapjacks	Rhubarb fruit cake
Passionate carrot cake	Fruit almond cake

Buffets

A buffet is a simple way of entertaining more people than will fit round your dinner table. Whether served at lunchtime or in the evening buffet food has to look good (colour is particularly important) as well as being tasty and well balanced. The selection below includes both hot and cold dishes that fulfil these criteria. Serve them with plenty of fresh wholemeal bread, rolls or specially-made black-bean, nut or soya breads. A selection of salads would go well with these dishes, but do not dress them too generously if your guests will be eating from paper plates.

Peanut croquettes	Sausages
Crusty field casserole	Spiced sausage casserole
Lentil slice	Hot sausage and potato salad
Macaroni flan	Crustless curried quiche
Crescent fish	Bacon leaf salad
Tuna mousse	Spinach nut ring
Baked fish slice	Avocado ring
Potted herrings	

Dinner

Dinner can be as simple or as elaborate as the occasion demands. Chapter 8 provides a good number of ideas for more formal occasions, while those listed below are intended as main-meal suggestions for everyday eating and entertaining. All have a good protein content and nutritional balance.

Poached egg curry, which, although complete in itself (not in need of a complementary protein) is good served with green baked rice

Fluffy green omelette, which, as eggs lack vitamin C, could be accompanied by a salad based on orange segments, peppers and watercress, for a light but well balanced supper

Savoury corn cake, another complete protein which could advantageously be balanced by a green vegetable dish

Cabbage nut korma, in which the nuts provide the protein, would be good served with one of the baked grain dishes, e.g. three-cooked wheat, millet pilaff or buckwheat slice

Levant filo, a fairly elaborate dish probably best embarked upon when entertaining, and ideally complemented with other foods from the region, e.g. a hummus starter and a Greek salad; curd cake would make an appropriate dessert

High-fibre meat loaf, bound to be a favourite with children, might be served with orange baked potatoes and perhaps tomato tower, which both have visual appeal

Paella, another dish suitable for entertaining, could be preceded by gazpacho and followed by fruit creams

Beef and lentil flan, which is very filling, is well balanced and needs nothing more than, for example, a little lightly creamed spinach; it is an ideal choice for quiet autumn suppers à deux

Marinated mango steaks, for a special dinner for two, might be served with stir-fried carrots; avocado mousse as a starter and summer pudding to follow would be appropriate

Green 'fried' lamb chops (page 59), could be served with a light potato salad dressed with yoghurt

Stuffed pork with cider, in need of no more than a green salad with dill dressing

Green toad, which contains a small amount of meat padded out with batter and greens, should be served with something colourful such as tomatoes

Ring of fish, a well-balanced dish that only needs a light vegetable accompaniment, such as 'simply beans' (page 89)

Coriander cod, another complete protein, delicious served with boiled brown rice

Tuna chicken casserole, served just with chunks of fresh, hot bread

Noodles with creamed sauce, which needs no specific accompaniment but could be served after a light soup for a more substantial meal

Marinated roast pork, which is a good dish to serve to those who think that a traditional roast is out of court in a healthy diet; serve with apple and cabbage slaw with dill dressing (the aniseed flavour of the dressing encourages digestion) and baked potatoes

Moroccan chicken, served with baked wheat and salad.

CHAPTER EIGHT

Entertaining ideas

The previous chapters of this book have outlined the principles of healthy eating and the practical means of preparing the food. Yet it is so easy, when confronted with the challenge of cooking to entertain, to cast aside one's healthy principles and revert to the old ways – fearful, perhaps, that without the butter and the double cream the meal might not be impressive or sophisticated enough to serve to friends.

In fact, there are plenty of recipes in the preceding chapters that would do justice to any dinner party, without giving the slightest impression that you are wearing a hair shirt under your Jean Muir. However, if further proof is needed, or you would feel happier with complete meal plans to show you how entertaining with a healthy slant can work, you need look no further. The thirteen menus, for both formal and informal occasions, are followed by suggestions for buffet meals, one-course entertaining, a one-dish supper meal, dinner dishes and fork suppers.

Menu 1

Green Pâté and home-made bread
Noodle Platter (see below) and Courgette Sambal
Pear and Yoghurt Custard Flan

This is an excellent way of introducing your guests to the tasty simplicity of 'new food'. Start with green pâté (see page 90) and home-made bread. For the main course, the noodle platter, cook the egg noodles, about 2 oz (50 g) dry weight per person, in boiling water until *al dente*. Steam a selection of vegetables, for example broccoli, carrots, mushrooms, courgettes, peppers and french beans.

Prepare a goulash- or saté-style sauce (see goulash recipe, page 164).

Assemble at the last minute, arranging the noodles on a flat oval or oblong serving dish and the vegetables in groups on top: for example, all the broccoli together at one end, all the beans at the other, with the carrots and pepper strips in the middle.

Carefully pour the prepared sauce over the middle, leaving some vegetables visible at the sides and ends. Garnish with fresh herbs: snipped fresh coriander is a good choice.

This dish, with its strong colour contrasts, makes a very attractive centrepiece, and the textures are wonderfully fresh and crunchy. Serve with courgette sambal (see page 94). To round off the meal, follow with pear and yoghurt custard flan (page 108).

Menu 2

An example of a vegetarian dinner-party menu for 4 that would satisfy the most dedicated meat-eater. (And remember that what you save by not buying meat can enable you to splash out a little more on special vegetarian ingredients.)

Egg and Tarragon Mousse
Asparagus Stack
Baked Vegetables
Orange Nut Crumble

Egg and tarragon mousse

SERVES 4

scant ¼ pint (125 ml) double cream
4 hard-boiled eggs
2 teaspoons (10 ml) vegetable setting
  agent
3 tablespoons (45 ml) water

4 tablespoons (60 ml) natural thick-set
  yoghurt
1 teaspoon (5 ml) tarragon
low-sodium worcestershire sauce
freshly ground black pepper
paprika

Whip the cream until stiff. Sieve the eggs, retaining four perfect slices for the garnish. Mix the eggs with the cream. Mix the setting agent with the cold water. Bring it to the boil, and boil gently for 2 minutes. Cool. Add to the cream mixture with all other ingredients except for the pepper and paprika. Pour into ramekins and smooth the surface of each. Chill for 2 hours before serving. Sprinkle black pepper over the top. Garnish each with an egg slice and top with a little paprika, for colour. Serve with hot wholemeal toast.

Asparagus stack

Short though its season is, asparagus is such a highly nutritious food that there are good reasons for finding new ways of serving it. Rich in vitamin E, it should never be boiled, because this destroys its nutrients. Light steaming is all that is necessary. These pancakes (see below) offer an alternative to serving asparagus in solitary splendour with a home-made dressing – delicious though that may be.

SERVES 4

4 oz (100 g) wholemeal flour	1½ oz (40 g) wholemeal flour
½ pint (250 ml) skimmed milk	1 oz (25 g) butter
2 eggs	¾ pint (375 ml) skimmed milk
SAUCE:	2 tablespoons (30 ml) white wine
8 oz (225 g) mushrooms, sliced	12 oz (350 g) asparagus, steamed

Liquidize the flour, milk and egg yolks. Whisk the egg whites until thick and fold into the flour mixture. Use the batter to make four pancakes in a lightly oiled non-stick frying-pan. Keep the pancakes warm.

For the sauce, oil a non-stick frying-pan and lightly sauté the mushrooms. Make a roux with the flour, butter and milk. Bring to the boil, add the wine and simmer. The sauce should be quite thick. Divide into two and add the mushrooms to one half. Carefully fold the asparagus into the other.

Lay one pancake on a serving dish and cover with half the mushroom sauce. Top with another pancake and cover with half the asparagus sauce. Continue until all the sauce is used up. Decorate with chopped parsley and serve cut into wedges, like a cake.

Baked vegetables

Cut a 4-inch (10-cm) square of tinfoil for each guest. Into each one place 1 slice of onion, a few peas, a small leek (chopped) and 1 thinly sliced carrot. Season with pepper and a sprinkling of lemon juice. Draw up the sides of the square round the vegetables and twist the edges to seal. Bake in a moderate oven, 375°F/190°C/Gas 5, for 20 minutes. Turn into individual dishes, dot with a spoonful of natural yoghurt and serve.

An exciting range of appetising 'mocktails' can be created from fresh fruits and vegetables.

Orange nut crumble

The use of sweet cecily, a fern-like herb smelling a little of aniseed, in this dish reduces the need for other sweeteners.

SERVES 4

1 lb (450g) apples
little water
sprig fresh sweet cecily
1 oz (25g) sultanas

3 oz (75g) butter
2 oz (50g) ground mixed nuts
4 oz (100g) wholemeal flour
1 orange

Peel and core the apples and place in non-stick saucepan with a little water and sweet cecily. Poach until soft. Remove the herb, drain and place the apples and sultanas in an ovenproof dish. Rub the fat and nuts into the flour. Peel the orange and extract the juice. Pour the juice over the other fruit. Mix a little chopped rind with the crumble topping and sprinkle the mixture over the fruit. Bake at 375°F/190°C/Gas 5 for about 25 minutes. Serve hot.

Menu 3

The starter/main course combinations in menus 3–13 provide bases for a range of entertaining situations, from formal dinner parties to after-theatre suppers. For the former, finish with a pudding from Chapter 5; for the latter, round off the meal by serving fresh fruit.

The first of these menus is for a dinner party for four.
Prawn Mouse with Avocado Sauce
Chicken Chip Pot

Vegetables and nuts combined with natural oils make tasty and well balanced salads.

Prawn mousse with avocado sauce

The smallest, cheapest prawns can be used for this
easy but impressive starter.

SERVES 4

8oz (225g) cottage cheese
¼ pint (150ml) natural low-fat yoghurt
3 teaspoons (15ml) vegetable setting agent
⅓ pint (180ml) vegetable stock
1 tablespoon (15ml) chopped fresh
  (not dried) parsley

freshly ground black pepper
4oz (100g) small cooked prawns, peeled
1 avocado, peeled and stoned
1 tablespoon (15ml) tomato juice
1 tablespoon (15ml) lemon juice

Sieve the cottage cheese or beat until smooth. Mix with the yoghurt.
Dissolve the setting agent in half the stock and mix with the cheese mixture.
Stir in the parsley, pepper and prawns. Spoon into four lightly oiled
ramekin dishes. Chill for 2 hours, until set. Liquidize the avocado with the
tomato juice, remaining stock and lemon juice until smooth.

When set, unmould each mousse into the centre of a small plate. Spoon a
thin layer of avocado sauce on to each plate, to surround the mousse.

Serve with sprouted soya bread (page 45).

Chicken chip pot

SERVES 4

8oz (225g) chick peas, soaked
1 lb (450g) potatoes, washed
8oz (225g) leeks, washed and sliced
4 chicken portions, skinned
1 tablespoon (15ml) marjoram
2 teaspoons (10ml) grain mustard

1 tablespoon (15ml) tomato purée
freshly ground black pepper
½ pint (300ml) stock
1 tablespoon (15ml)
  polyunsaturated margarine
paprika

Cook the chick peas in boiling water for about 1½ hours until soft.
Drain. Meanwhile, cut the potatoes into thick matchsticks. Place half the
chick peas and leeks in a deep casserole. Arrange the chicken pieces on
top. Cover with the remaining leeks and peas.

Arrange the potato 'chips' vertically in the top of the casserole so they
stick upwards like trees. Mix the marjoram, mustard, tomato purée,
pepper and stock together. Pour over the casserole. Dot the potatoes with
the margarine and sprinkle paprika over the top. Bake at 375°F/190°C/
Gas 5 for 30 minutes, or until the chips are crisp and golden.

If preferred, omit the margarine, which serves mainly to give the
potatoes a better finish.

Menu 4

This makes a light lunch or supper for two.
Baked Squash
Sole Véronique

Baked squash

This vegetable starter, which is both delicious and very simple
to prepare, balances well with the fish main course.
It is best eaten with a grapefruit spoon.

SERVES 2

1 acorn squash between two
1 tablespoon (15ml) olive oil per
  squash

2 tablespoons (30ml) lemon juice per
  squash
1 clove garlic, crushed
freshly ground black pepper

Cut the squash horizontally in two, and scoop out the seeds and fibrous
material in the middle. Put the oil, lemon juice, garlic and pepper into the
cavity. Wrap in tinfoil and bake in the oven at 375°F/190°C/Gas 5 for 20–25
minutes until soft. Serve hot.

Sole véronique

SERVES 2

1½ lb (700g) sole (or plaice) fillets
1 small onion, chopped
2 tablespoons (30ml) lemon juice
freshly ground black pepper
1 bay leaf
¼ pint (150ml) dry French white wine

6oz (175g) grapes, halved and de-seeded
½ tablespoon (7.5ml)
  polyunsaturated margarine
scant ½ tablespoon (7.5ml)
  wholemeal flour
¼ pint (150ml) natural low-fat yoghurt

Lightly oil a casserole dish. Add the fish, onion, lemon juice, pepper, bay
leaf and wine. Cover and bake at 350°F/180°C/Gas 4 for 10–15 minutes.
Drain off the liquid and reserve. Discard the bay leaf. Add all but a few
grapes to the fish and keep warm.

In a separate pan melt the margarine, stir in the flour and ½ pint (300ml)
of the fish liquor. Cook until smooth and thickened. Remove from the
heat. Stir in the yoghurt. Heat through, without boiling. Pour the sauce
carefully over the fish. Garnish with the reserved grapes and serve with
boiled brown rice.

This is a substantial supper menu.
Sesame Fish
Pork Gnocchi

Sesame fish

This starter would also be suitable for a more elaborate dinner party.

SERVES 2–3

12 oz (350g) white fish fillets, e.g. coley	*2 oz (50g) sesame seeds*
6 teaspoons (30ml) fish masala (see page 77)	*4 fl oz (100ml) natural low-fat yoghurt*
1 clove garlic, crushed	*2 teaspoons (10ml) tandoori paste*
1 small egg, beaten	*2 tablespoons (30ml) coriander leaves*

Completely bone and skin the fish. Cut into bite-sized pieces. In a bowl combine the masala, garlic and egg. Drop the fish into the mixture and leave for 1 hour. Spread the sesame seeds on a board. Remove the fish from the marinade and coat on each side with seeds. Place the pieces on a lightly oiled non-stick baking tray. Bake at 400°F/200°C/Gas 6 for 15 minutes until crisp and brown.

Meanwhile, make the sauce by combining the yoghurt with the tandoori paste. Serve the fish with the sauce, garnished with coriander leaves. An extra garnish of lime slices would be attractive.

Pork gnocchi

SERVES 2–3

½ teaspoon (2.5ml) grated nutmeg	*1 onion, chopped*
1 pint (600ml) skimmed milk	*2 cloves garlic, crushed*
freshly ground black pepper	*1 oz (25g) polyunsaturated margarine*
4 oz (100g) fine wholemeal semolina	*1 tablespoon (15ml) sage*
3 oz (75g) low-fat Cheddar, grated	*8 oz (225g) mushrooms, quartered*
1 egg, whisked	*paprika*
12 oz (350g) lean pork, cut into small cubes	

Make the gnocchi topping at least 2 hours in advance, by boiling the milk, nutmeg and pepper together in a saucepan and adding the semolina away from the heat. Stir in and return to the boil. Simmer for 5 minutes until very thick. Remove from the heat. Add the cheese and egg. Beat well.

Return to the heat and cook gently for a few minutes more. Oil a large shallow dish and spread the gnocchi mixture in it evenly. Leave in the refrigerator to become completely cold and set.

In a non-stick frying-pan sauté the pork with the onion and garlic in the margarine. Add the sage and mushrooms. Keep stirring to prevent sticking. Continue until the meat is cooked and the mushrooms release their juices (about 20 minutes).

Transfer the meat mixture to a shallow ovenproof dish. Cut the gnocchi topping into squares and overlap them, 'cobbler' fashion, on the meat. Sprinkle with paprika and grill until bubbling and browned.

Menu 6

This is an elegant but not too formal dinner-party menu.
Egg and Cucumber Mousse
Spinach Pork Parcel with Orange Baked Potatoes and Grainy Cottage Cheese Slice
New Mont Blanc (page 107)

Egg and cucumber mousse

SERVES 4

½ pint (300ml) skimmed milk

1 small onion, minced

parsley sprigs

1 bay leaf

6 peppercorns

blade of mace

1 oz (25g) polyunsaturated margarine

1 oz (25g) wholemeal flour

4 oz (100g) cottage cheese

¼ pint (150ml) natural low-fat yoghurt

4 hard-boiled eggs, chopped

2-inch (5-cm) piece of cucumber, chopped and left to drain

1 tablespoon (15ml) worcestershire sauce

½ oz (15g) vegetable setting agent

2 tablespoons (30ml) cold water

watercress

Infuse the milk with the onion, parsley, bay leaf, peppercorns and mace. Bring to the boil and leave for 10 minutes. Discard all the ingredients except the milk and onion. Melt the margarine and add the flour. Make up the white sauce using the infused milk. When the sauce is cool beat in the cottage cheese, yoghurt, eggs, cucumber and worcestershire sauce.

Mix the setting agent in the water and heat gently. Mix with the other ingredients. Pour the mousse mixture into a lightly oiled mould (a soufflé dish or a ring mould, or individual ramekins). Cover and place in the refrigerator for 6 hours until set. Unmould and garnish with sprigs of watercress. Serve with a French granary stick.

Spinach pork parcel

SERVES 4

12 oz (350 g) pork, minced	freshly ground black pepper
1 onion, chopped	4 oz (100 g) mushrooms, sliced
2 cloves garlic, crushed	2 tomatoes, chopped
1 tablespoon (15 ml) paprika	1 tablespoon (15 ml) grain mustard
2 teaspoons (10 ml) ground	2 oz (50 g) oats
cumin	1 lb (450 g) spinach leaves, washed
dash Tabasco sauce	4 oz (100 g) Edam, grated

Sauté the mince in a non-stick frying-pan. Add the onion, garlic, spices, Tabasco, pepper and mushrooms. Stir in the tomatoes, mustard and oats.

Lightly oil a shallow, oblong ovenproof dish. Line with about half the spinach leaves, overlapping them on the bottom and sides of the dish. Spoon in the meat mixture. Sprinkle with half the cheese. Cover with the rest of the spinach leaves. Sprinkle on the remaining cheese. Cover with tinfoil and bake at 400°F/200°C/Gas 6 for 45 minutes.

Serve with orange baked potatoes and grainy buckwheat slice.

Menu 7

For a light, informal supper this filling soup and unusual fish dish are ideal. Serve lots of fresh home-made wholemeal rolls through the meal. The suggested dessert may of course be made well in advance, to be ready and waiting.

Grandmother's Potato Soup

Haddock in Bok Choi with Lentil Salad or Jeddrah

Passionate Carrot Cake (page 112)

Grandmother's potato soup

SERVES 2

1 onion, chopped	1 pig's trotter
1 leek, chopped and cleaned	2 pints (1 litre) stock
1 tablespoon (15 ml) olive oil	1 teaspoon (5 ml) low-salt
1 carrot, chopped and	yeast extract
scrubbed	freshly ground black pepper
4 cleaned potatoes, quartered	chervil

Sauté the onion and leek in oil in a large saucepan. Add the carrot and potatoes and mix well. Add the trotter, cut into four. Pour on the stock, mixed with the yeast extract. Bring to the boil and simmer over a very low heat for about 2 hours. Top up the stock if necessary during cooking. Remove the trotter. Season with pepper. Serve garnished with chervil leaves.

Haddock in bok choi

SERVES 2

8–10 large, outer leaves of bok choi or
    Chinese cabbage
1 lb (450 g) haddock fillets
1 teaspoon (5 ml) fennel seeds,
    slightly crushed

1 teaspoon (5 ml) paprika
4 mushrooms, thinly sliced
4 spring onions, chopped

Turn the Chinese leaves face down and run your thumb down the stems to break the spines. Line an oiled shallow ovenproof dish with leaves, stem-side inwards, overlapping the sides.

Lay the fish fillets in the dish, sprinkle with fennel seeds and paprika and lay the mushrooms in neat rows over the top. Sprinkle over the onion. Fold in the leaves to cover. Cover and bake in the oven at 400°F/200°C/Gas 6 for 30 minutes.

Serve with lentil salad or jeddrah (see below).

Lentil salad

This delicious salad is very simple to make and is high in fibre and vitamins.

SERVES 2

8 oz (225 g) whole small brown
    lentils, cooked
1 small onion, chopped
½ teaspoon (2.5 ml) ground
    cumin
½ teaspoon (2.5 ml) ground
    coriander

large bunch continental
    parsley, finely chopped
2 oz (50 g) cracked wheat, soaked
2 tablespoons (30 ml) oil and lemon
    dressing with garlic
2 tablespoons (30 ml) natural low-
    fat yoghurt
freshly ground black pepper

In a large serving bowl combine the lentils with the onion and spices. Add the parsley and wheat. Stir in the dressing and yoghurt. Season liberally with pepper and serve lightly chilled.

Jeddrah

This Middle-Eastern dish is both simple to make and extremely tasty, and can be served either as a starter or as a side dish with a main course. It would also make a good supper dish for two served with a mixed salad and warm wholemeal pitta.

SERVES 2–4

4 oz (100 g) split lentils, soaked for about 1 hour
2 oz (50 g) bulgar wheat
1 onion, chopped
1 tablespoon (15 ml) olive oil

1 tablespoon (15 ml) pine nuts
lemon juice (optional)
freshly ground pepper (optional)
celery leaves, chopped

Cook the lentils in ½ pint (300 ml) boiling water for about 30 minutes, until softened but still whole and separate. Add the bulgar wheat to the cooked lentils in their pan and leave until the water is absorbed (about 20 minutes). The mixture should be quite dry.

Sauté the onion in the oil with the pine nuts. Mix into the lentil mixture. Season with a little lemon juice and black pepper, if liked, and top with celery leaves.

Note This dish can be made in advance, turned into a gratin dish and topped with tomatoes. Re-heat in a hot oven and serve immediately.

Menu 8

This is an unusual menu for a formal family dinner.
Tomato Soup with sesame crackers
Sweet Potato Prawn Cakes
Mushroom Barley

Sweet potato prawn cakes

SERVES 4

2 oz (50 g) wholemeal flour
pinch vegetable seasoning
1 4–6-oz (100–175-g) sweet potato
   scrubbed
4 oz (100 g) pumpkin, grated

4 oz (100 g) prawns
1 oz (25 g) arrowroot
olive oil
1 tablespoon (15 ml) coriander

Mix together the flour and vegetable seasoning. Grate the vegetables, chop the prawns, combine all the ingredients except the coriander and mix together well. They should stick together (if, after thorough mixing, they do not, add a small egg at this stage and mix again). Shape the vegetable mixture into round, flattish cakes, like burgers.

Oil a non-stick frying-pan. Fry each cake for 5 minutes on each side until crisp and brown on the outside. Garnish with coriander leaves.

Serve with a warm garlic-flavoured sauce, such as skordalia (page 91) and accompany with mushroom barley (see below) and a leaf salad.

Mushroom barley

SERVES 4

8 oz (225 g) barley, washed
1¼ pints (750 ml) vegetable stock
8 oz (225 g) mushrooms
1 tablespoon (15 ml) olive oil

freshly ground black pepper
paprika
flat-leaved parsley

Cook the barley in the stock until the liquid is absorbed (about 1 hour). Sauté the mushrooms in the oil. Add the pepper and paprika and combine with the well-drained barley. Mix thoroughly and place in a serving dish. Garnish with the parsley and serve.

Menu 9

This is ideal for Saturday lunch.
Beef Scone Round with green cabbage slaw or other salad

Beef scone round

This is a healthier alternative to the ubiquitous pizza.

SERVES 4

8 oz (225 g) lean beef, minced
1 onion, chopped
2 cloves garlic, crushed
8 oz (225 g) borlotti beans, cooked
4 oz (100 g) sweetcorn, cooked
1 lb (450 g) tomatoes, chopped
2 tablespoons (30 ml) tomato purée
1 teaspoon (5 ml) ground cumin

freshly ground black pepper
8 oz (225 g) wholemeal flour
4 teaspoons (20 ml) baking powder
½ teaspoon (2.5 ml) turmeric
2 oz (50 g) polyunsaturated margarine
¼ pint (150 ml) buttermilk
4 oz (100 g) low-fat Cheddar, grated

Dry-fry the mince in a non-stick frying-pan until browned. Add the onions and garlic. Stir in the beans, sweetcorn, tomatoes, purée, cumin and pepper. Cook until thickened to a sauce.

Mix the flour and baking powder with the turmeric. Rub in the fat. Stir in the buttermilk to form a soft, dryish, dough. Knead well in the bowl, then form into a large round about the size of a dinner-plate. Spread the beef mixture on top, spreading just short of the edge. Sprinkle over the cheese and bake at 425°F/220°C/Gas 7 for 20 minutes until the dough is well risen and cooked through. Serve cut into wedges.

This is good accompanied by a crisp, shredded green salad, for example, a green cabbage slaw or brussels sprouts-based salad.

Menu 10

This is a good dinner-party menu.
Stilton-stuffed Pears and Boiled Black-bean Bread
Brunswick Stew
Cardinals' Hats (see page 120)

Brunswick stew

SERVES 4

4 chicken or rabbit portions,
  skinned
1½ pints (900 ml) stock, made with a
  low-salt cube
1 large onion, sliced
pinch cayenne pepper
1 tablespoon (15 ml) worcestershire
  sauce
½ teaspoon (2.5 ml) dried thyme

½ teaspoon (2.5 ml) dried oregano
2 medium potatoes, cleaned and
  diced
8 oz (225 g) shelled broad beans
1 lb (450 g) tomatoes, chopped
8 oz (225 g) sweetcorn
2 thick slices wholemeal or granary
  bread
freshly ground black pepper

Put the meat, stock, onion, cayenne pepper, worcestershire sauce and herbs in a saucepan and bring to the boil. Reduce the heat and simmer until cooked (about 30 minutes).

Add the potatoes, beans, tomatoes and corn. Simmer for a further 20 minutes. Cut the bread into neat cubes. Add to the stew, with the black pepper, and cook for a further 10 minutes while the stew thickens slightly. Serve in deep plates.

Note Rabbit is low in cholesterol and very tasty in this dish. If you use chicken is must be skinned (most of the fat resides in its skin); not only is this fat unhealthy and unnecessary but it would leave the stew with an oily coating.

Menu 11

A Sunday-evening supper menu that makes full use of vegetables and fruit.
Falafel
Red Chicken

Falafel

Serve small portions as a starter or, as a main course, serve
with salad in wholemeal pitta. This makes a good lunch dish
accompanied by creamed tahini sauce.

SERVES 4

8 oz (225 g) chick peas
1 onion, chopped
1 clove garlic, pressed
2 oz (50 g) parsley, chopped
pinch chilli seasoning

1 teaspoon (5 ml) ground coriander
1 teaspoon (5 ml) ground cumin
freshly ground black pepper
2 tablespoons (30 ml) lemon juice
olive oil

Cook the chick peas in boiling water until well cooked (about 2 hours, unless you have a pressure cooker, in which case follow the manufacturers' instructions). Drain. Grind in a food processor with the onion and garlic. Add the remaining ingredients, except for the oil.

Shape the mixture into balls, then flatten. Put a little oil into a non-stick saucepan and heat. Put the falafel into a pan, allowing room to turn them, and cook for 8–10 minutes until cooked through. Repeat until the mixture is used up.

Alternatively, cook in the oven, turning once, for 30 minutes at 400°F/200°C/Gas 6.

The falafel should be crisp outside and soft and grainy inside.

Traditionally falafel are deep-fried, so this recipe is a more healthful deviation.

Red chicken

SERVES 4

4 chicken portions, skinned
1 onion, chopped
½oz (15g) wholemeal flour
1 teaspoon (5ml) ground ginger

8oz (225g) rhubarb, cleaned and chopped
¼ pint (150ml) white wine
   (preferably German)
2 sprigs sweet cecily, in whole pieces

In a non-stick frying-pan brown the chicken with the onion. Gently sauté for 15 minutes. Transfer the chicken to an ovenproof dish. Add the flour, ginger and rhubarb to the pan. Stir and add the wine. Add the herbs and cook gently until the rhubarb is cooked and the mixture is reduced to thick, smooth, sauce-like consistency.

Remove the herb pieces and pour the sauce over the chicken. Bake at 375°F/190°C/Gas 5 for 15 minutes. Serve hot and bubbling with chunky granary bread.

Menu 12

This is another supper menu.
Flowers of the Field
Ratatouille Meat Pie

Flowers of the field

This is not a dish for those who do not like onions, but it is wonderfully healthful for those that do. It is based on a medieval recipe and makes a good, simple first course accompanied by wholemeal bread, followed by ratatouille meat pie (see below).

SERVES 4

1lb (450g) small button onions,
   peeled
1oz (25g) butter
1 tablespoon (15ml) wholemeal flour

½ pint (300ml) low-fat skimmed
   milk
4 hard-boiled eggs, halved
2oz (50g) flaked almonds

Blanch the onions. Make up a white sauce with the butter, flour and milk. Place one egg in the bottom off each of four ramekin dishes. Divide the onions equally between dishes. Pour over the sauce. Garnish with the almonds.

Bake at 375°F/190°C/Gas 5 for 20 minutes until the sauce is bubbling and the almonds are browned.

Ratatouille meat pie

2 onions, sliced
3 cloves garlic
1 teaspoon (5 ml) olive oil
8 oz (225 g) tomatoes, chopped
1 green pepper, cut into medium-
  sized pieces
1 small aubergine, sliced
8 oz (225 g) lean pork, minced

1 tablespoon (15 ml) tomato purée
1 tablespoon (15 ml) marjoram
2 teapoons (10 ml) mustard powder
2 oz (50 g) wholemeal flour
2 teaspoons (10 ml) ground coriander
few drops soy sauce
2 oz (50 g) fine oatmeal
1 small egg, beaten

Soften the onion and 1 clove of garlic in 1 teaspoon (5 ml) olive oil in a non-stick frying-pan. Add the remainder of the vegetables and cook over a low heat until they are glossy and beginning to soften but still crisp. Crush the other 2 garlic cloves. Mix together in a bowl the meat, tomato purée, herbs, mustard, flour, spice, soy sauce and oatmeal. Beat in the eggs.

Use two-thirds of the meat mixture to line a small deep pie-dish. Using a slotted spoon, fill the meat lining with the ratatouille mixture. Use the remainder of the meat mixture to make a 'lid'. Bake at 350°F/180°C/Gas 4 for 1 hour. Serve accompanied by corn pop-ups (page 57).

Menu 13

This is a dinner-party menu.
Chinese Lettuce Baskets
Poulet Parcels and Moroccan Vegetable Grain Bake

Chinese lettuce baskets

This makes an excellent starter, and can be easily expanded to feed larger numbers.

4 lettuce leaves (ideally iceberg,
  otherwise Webb's, as these must
  be completely whole
  and bowl-shaped)
1 tablespoon (15 ml) olive oil
1 small piece fresh ginger, finely
  chopped
1 clove garlic, chopped

4 eggs
¼ teaspoon (1 ml) five-spice powder
4 small leeks or large spring onions,
  well washed and chopped
4 slices carrot
freshly ground black pepper
Chinese parsley or coriander leaves
  to garnish

Clean and dry the lettuce and set on individual plates. Heat the oil in a wok or frying-pan. Add the ginger and garlic and stir-fry for 2 minutes. Whisk the egg with 2 tablespoons (30 ml) water and the five-spice powder. Add the leeks to the oil in the wok or pan and stir-fry until they start to soften. Add the eggs to the leek mixture and quickly scramble.

Cut the carrot slices into decorative petal-shapes. Divide the egg mixture equally between the lettuce cups. Season with pepper. Garnish with the carrot pieces and top with parsley or coriander leaves. Serve while still warm.

Poulet parcels

SERVES 4

4 chicken breasts, skinned, boned and slightly beaten to flatten	2 teaspoons (10 ml) wholemeal flour
8 oz (225 g) smoked haddock fillets, skinned, boned and chopped	2 teaspoons (10 ml) lemon juice
	4 fl oz (100 ml) white wine
4 cloves garlic, crushed	4 fl oz (100 ml) natural low-fat yoghurt
1 teaspoon (5 ml) dill seeds	4 oz (100 g) prawns
freshly ground black pepper	4 oz (100 g) button mushrooms, thinly sliced
small bunch chives, snipped	dill weed to garnish
½ oz (15 g) polyunsaturated margarine	

Lay the chicken breasts in an ovenproof dish. Mix the boned and chopped fish in a bowl with the garlic, dill seeds, black pepper and chives. Divide the mixture into four and place a quarter on each chicken breast. Fold the chicken over the filling, keeping the joins underneath. Bake in the oven at 375°F/190°C/Gas 5 for 30 minutes.

For the sauce, melt the margarine in a pan and stir in the flour. Drain any liquid from the chicken breast dish and blend it into the flour. Return the chicken to the oven. Add the lemon juice and white wine to the sauce. When thickened, add the yoghurt gradually. Add the prawns, stirring continuously. When the chicken is cooked, place the mushroom slices over each fillet and carefully spoon over the sauce. Garnish with dill weed.

Serve straight away, with Moroccan vegetable grain bake.

Moroccan vegetable grain bake

2 tablespoons (30ml) oil

3 medium onions, 2 sliced
  and 1 diced

2 cloves garlic, crushed

3 tablespoons (45 ml) red lentils

8oz (225g) brown rice

1½ pints (900ml) water

1lb (450g) spinach, thoroughly
  cleaned and dried

1 level tablespoon (15ml) ground
  coriander

freshly ground black pepper

1 teaspoon (5ml) chopped mint

2 tablespoons (30ml) chopped fresh
  flat-leaved parsley

8fl oz (225ml) natural low-fat
  yoghurt

Heat two-thirds of the oil in a saucepan and sauté the sliced onions and the garlic until lightly browned. Stir in the lentils and rice. Add the water, bring to the boil, reduce the heat and simmer for 20 minutes. Add the spinach, coriander and pepper. Cook for a further 25 minutes.

Meanwhile sauté the third onion in the remaining oil until well browned. Sprinkle on the mint and stir well. Transfer the cooked rice mixture to a serving bowl and stir in the parsley. Stir in the yoghurt. Sprinkle the fried onion mixture over the rice.

This dish may be kept warm until ready to serve.

The natural sweetness and high fibre content of dried fruits make them one of the most useful elements in a healthy diet.

Creamy pancake roll

This could be made in advance.

1 tablespoon (15 ml) olive oil

2 oz (50 g) wholemeal flour

1 large egg

¼ pint (150 ml) low-fat skimmed milk

1 chicken or turkey breast, minced (or cooked leftovers)

1 onion, chopped

1 clove garlic, minced

1 heaped tablespoon (20 ml) wholemeal flour

½ pint (300 ml) skimmed milk

2 oz (50 g) sweetcorn, blanched

1 tablespoon (15 ml) chopped tarragon

4 mushrooms, sliced

1 tablespoon (15 ml) ground almonds

freshly ground black pepper

Blend the oil, flour, egg and milk in a liquidizer. Leave to rest. Grease a non-stick swiss-roll tin and place in the oven at 475°F/240°C/Gas 9 to heat. Pour in the pancake batter and cook for 10 minutes until firm and golden. Turn out on to greaseproof paper and cover with a clean tea-towel.

Grease a non-stick frying-pan and sauté the minced meat with the onion and garlic until the vegetables are transparent. Add the flour and stir in the milk. Add the sweetcorn, tarragon and mushrooms, and, if using cooked leftovers, the meat. Stir and remove from heat. The mixture should be smooth but well thickened.

Spread the mixture over the pancake and roll up like a swiss roll. Sprinkle the roll with the ground almonds and pepper and return to the oven at 350°F/180°C/Gas 4 for 20 minutes.

Butter beans, cooked with tomatoes and combined with red onions, garlic and coriander, are delicious served either hot or cold.

Spinach lentil bake

This is a hot dish.

SERVES 4

1lb (450g) spinach
4oz (100g) lean meat, minced
1 onion, chopped
1 tablespoon (15ml) mustard
  powder
2 cloves garlic, crushed
1 teaspoon (5ml) cumin seeds
1 tablespoon (15ml) tomato purée

freshly ground black pepper
1 teaspoon (5ml) savory leaves
8oz (225g) continental lentils
1 tablespoon (15ml) oil
¼ pint (150ml) natural low-fat
  yoghurt
4 tomatoes, sliced
4oz (100g) low-fat Cheddar, grated

Wash, cook and drain the spinach. Sauté the meat in a non-stick frying-pan with the onion, mustard, garlic, cumin, tomato purée, pepper and savory. Cook the lentils in 1 pint (600ml) water. Drain and leave to dry out.

Place the spinach in an ovenproof dish or divide between four individual ovenproof dishes. Spread the mince over the spinach evenly.

In a separate bowl combine the lentils with the oil, yoghurt and more pepper. Spread the topping over the mince mixture, arrange the tomato slices round the edge and sprinkle over the cheese. Bake at 400°F/200°C/Gas 6 for 25 minutes until the topping is golden brown.

Apricot pilaff

SERVES 4

8oz (225g) wheat berries, soaked
2 tablespoons (30ml) vegetable oil
small piece fresh ginger, chopped
3 cloves garlic, crushed
1 onion, chopped
1 teaspoon (5ml) cumin seeds
3oz (75g) dried apricots, soaked and
  chopped

1 teaspoon (5ml) celery seeds
4oz (100g) pine nuts
1 pint (600ml) vegetable stock
2 tomatoes, chopped
freshly ground black pepper
fresh coriander leaves to garnish

Sauté the wheat in the oil in a non-stick saucepan. Add the ginger, garlic and onion. After a few minutes add the cumin seeds. Drain the apricots and add to the pan with the celery seeds. Add the pine nuts and the stock. Bring to the boil and simmer for about 40 minutes until the wheat is cooked and fully puffed up (add more stock or water if necessary to prevent drying out). Stir in the tomatoes and pepper. Garnish with the coriander leaves and serve.

Toad-in-the-hole

By changing some of the ingredients in the traditional recipe
a delicious but healthful alternative has been devised.

SERVES 4

8oz (225g) lean beef, minced
2oz (50g) soft wholemeal
  breadcrumbs
2oz (50g) oatmeal
1 onion, chopped
1 teaspoon (5ml) marjoram
1 tablespoon (15ml) tomato
  purée
good dash worcestershire sauce

freshly ground black pepper
1 tablespoon (15ml) chopped
  parsley
1 tablespoon (5ml) vegetable
  seasoning
4oz (100g) wholemeal flour
1 egg, whisked
½ pint (300ml) low-fat skimmed
  milk

In a mixing bowl combine the first ten ingredients to form the meatball
mixture. Form into balls and place in a non-stick roasting-tin. Bake at
425°F/220°C/Gas 7 for 20 minutes.

Meanwhile, in a liquidizer, combine the flour, egg and milk. When the
meatballs are cooked, pour the batter mixture over the top and cook for a
further 20 minutes until well risen and golden.

Hot Indian salad is an ideal accompaniment (page 98).

Mediterranean fish casserole

1 lb (450g) coley, boned, skinned and
   cut into bite-sized pieces
1 mackerel, gutted, filleted and cut
   into pieces
6oz (75g) peeled prawns
2 onions, sliced
1 green pepper, de-seeded and sliced
2 cloves garlic, crushed
1 tablespoon (15ml) tarragon

1 tablespoon (15ml) chopped
   parsley
1 bay leaf
freshly ground black pepper
6 tomatoes, chopped
½ pint (150ml) white wine
2 slices wholemeal bread
1 tablespoon (15ml) French
   mustard

Put the fish in an ovenproof casserole covered by onions, green pepper, garlic and herbs. Season. Add the tomatoes and wine. Cover and cook in the oven at 375°F/190°C/Gas 5 for 30 minutes.

Meanwhile toast the bread. Spread with the mustard and cut into triangles. When the casserole is ready, decorate with the bread and garnish with more parsley, if liked.

Note To vary, if liked, and subject to the availability of fresh supplies, add mussels and cockles, which are both cheap and nutritious. Prepare and cook, then add to the casserole along with the prawns. Another possible addition is cooked haricot beans, for a more substantial dish.

Serve accompanied by, for example, green rice bake (page 93).

Chicken goulash

This is a lighter alternative to the traditional beef goulash – chicken is lower in saturated fats – and the wholemeal noodle accompaniment will increase the fibre content too.

2 tablespoons (30ml) wholemeal
   flour
1 tablespoon (15ml) paprika
1 tablespoon (15ml) caraway seeds
freshly ground black pepper
2 chicken breasts, skinned and cubed
1 onion, chopped
4 carrots, scrubbed, not peeled, and
   chopped
1 red pepper, de-seeded and sliced

1 green pepper, de-seeded and sliced
4oz (100g) mushrooms, sliced
8oz (225g) tomatoes, sliced
¼ pint (150ml) tomato juice
¼ pint (150ml) low-salt stock
¼ pint (150ml) red wine
2 tablespoons (30ml) tomato purée
½ pint (300ml) natural thick-set
   low-fat yoghurt
parsley leaves to garnish

Season the flour with the paprika, caraway seeds and black pepper and place in a bag. Add the chicken pieces one at a time and coat. Carefully arrange the chicken in a casserole. Add the vegetables. Combine all the liquids, except the yoghurt, with any remaining flour and stir in the purée. Pour over the casserole.

Bake in the oven at 350°F/180°C/Gas 4 for 1½ hours. Stir in the yoghurt, garnish with parsley and serve over cooked wholemeal noodles.

A dish of sprouted beans with yoghurt dill dressing makes a tasty accompaniment.

Chinese steamed chicken

This steamed dish allows the natural flavours of
the food to be appreciated.

SERVES 2

large piece stem ginger, cut into
  three
2 cloves garlic, crushed
1 lb (450g) broccoli spears
8oz (225g) chicken fillets, sliced
  paper-thin

½ teaspoon (2.5 ml) five-spice
  powder
12 oz (350g) wholemeal spaghetti
5 fl oz (150 ml) natural low-fat
  yoghurt
soy sauce

In a large saucepan, bring 2 pints (1 litre) water to the boil. Add two-thirds of the ginger, chopped, and 1 clove garlic. Set the steamer over boiling water with the broccoli on one side and the very thinly sliced chicken on the other. Sprinkle the five-spice powder over the chicken. Steam for 10 minutes or until tender.

Meanwhile cook the spaghetti in boiling water. In a separate bowl combine the yoghurt, other garlic clove and remaining pieces of ginger, minced, with the soy sauce. Drain the spaghetti and arrange on a large serving platter. Lay the broccoli over the top in the centre and arrange the cooked chicken slices over the top. Dribble a little of the sauce over the dish and serve the rest separately.

Serve with triple-cooked wheat (page 52).

Arabic beef breads

These are very good for a light lunch party. The breads can be
made in advance and filled as required.

SERVES 6

1 large onion, minced

4 oz (100 g) lean beef, ground

*4 tablespoons (60 ml) chopped
    coriander leaves*

2 teaspoons (10 ml) ground cumin

*½ teaspoon (2.5 ml) ground
    cinnamon*

½ teaspoon (2.5 ml) chilli seasoning

dash worcestershire sauce

4 oz (100 g) wholemeal flour

tomato juice (optional)

olive oil

Mix the onion and beef with the coriander and seasonings. Mix in the
flour and if necessary a little tomato juice to make the mixture stick
together (different flours absorb different amounts of liquid). Mix together
for about 5 minutes. Divide the dough into balls about the size of a golf
ball and with floured hands flattened out as thinly as possible. Chill in the
refrigerator.

In a non-stick frying-pan as near as possible to the size of the flattened
dough, heat only just enough oil to cover the bottom (it will spread evenly
as it warms). When hot, cook the dough on one side, then turn and brown
the other side. Drain on kitchen paper. Repeat until all the dough is used
up.

Fold each bread in half and serve filled with tomato and onion salad,
sprinkled with oregano and topped with yoghurt.

Alternatively, leave flat and pile on a mixture of bean sprouts and chick
peas in a sweet-and-sour salad dressing.

One-dish supper meal

Bobotie

This dish, with its typically South African flavour, would be
enhanced by the accompaniment of a good dry and flinty South African
wine, possibly mixed half and half with mineral water.

1lb (450g) lean minced beef	3 tablespoons (45ml) lemon juice
2 large onions, sliced	freshly ground black pepper
1 apple, cored and sliced, but not peeled	2 bay leaves
1 tablespoon (15 ml) curry powder	1 egg
2oz (50g) sultanas	¼ pint (150ml) low-fat skimmed milk
2oz (50g) flaked almonds	good pinch garam masala

Sauté the beef in a non-stick frying-pan. Drain off any excess oil. Add the onion to the meat and brown. Add the apple and stir. Stir in the curry powder, sultanas and half the almonds. Mix in the lemon juice and pepper. Transfer to a shallow ovenproof dish and add the bay leaves. Bake at 350°F/180°C/Gas 4 for 45 minutes. Remove from the oven.

Whisk the egg and milk together. Pour the milk mixture over the dish and sprinkle the remaining almonds on top with the garam masala.

Return to the oven for a further 10 minutes at 400°F/200°C/Gas 6 until the topping is set.

Dinner dishes

The section that follows is for healthy main-meal dishes.

Soaked fish

1 lb (450g) plaice, skinned and filleted	4 tablespoons (60ml) lemon juice
1 carrot, cut into julienne strips	2 tablespoons (30ml) olive oil
	1 fresh chilli, sliced
	freshly ground black pepper
1 onion, cut into rings	1 green pepper, cut into rings

Cut the filleted fish into strips and place in an ovenproof dish. Put the carrot and onion over the top. Pour over the lemon and oil. Add the sliced chilli and a generous amount of black pepper. Cook in the oven at 425°F/220°C/Gas 7 for 10 minutes. Allow to soak in the dressing in the dish until required (at least 2 hours) and serve, garnished with pepper rings, accompanied by generous chunks of black bread.

Peanut peachy chicken

To make a substantial meal (and provide an appetizing colour contrast) serve this chicken dish with spinach pudding.

SERVES 4

2 teaspoons (10ml) ground cumin
3oz (75 g) salt-free peanut butter
1 tablespoon (15ml) lemon juice
freshly ground black pepper
4 chicken pieces, skinned

1 small onion, cut into thick slices
4 small peaches, halved and
   stoned but not peeled
lovage leaves

Mix the cumin with the peanut butter, lemon juice and pepper to taste. Line a grill pan with tinfoil. Lay the chicken pieces on the foil and spread half the seasoning mixture over the top. Grill gently for about 15 minutes, roughening the topping from time to time to prevent burning. Turn the chicken and add the rest of mixture to the uncooked side.

Repeat the grilling process. Add the onion slices and peach halves for the last 5 minutes of cooking.

Serve with a topping of onion rings and peach halves, garnished with lovage leaves.

Beef oat crumble

Children usually enjoy this dish.

SERVES 2

8oz (225g) lean beef, minced
1 onion, chopped
2 cloves garlic, chopped
pinch ground nutmeg
freshly ground black pepper
pinch ground coriander
1 tablespoon (15ml) marjoram

4oz (100g) haricot beans, cooked
8oz (225g) tomatoes, chopped
2 tablespoons (30ml) tomato purée
several outside leaves cabbage or
   other greens
soy sauce, to taste
4oz (100g) oat topping (see below)

Brown the meat well in a non-stick saucepan. Add the onion and garlic. Sauté with the spices and herbs. Add the beans, tomatoes and purée. Cook until a thick consistency is achieved. Shred the cabbage and add to the pan with the soy sauce. Turn into an ovenproof casserole and sprinkle the oat topping on top. Bake at 375°F/190°C/Gas 5 for 30 minutes until brown.

Oat topping

4 oz (100 g) rolled oats
2 oz (50 g) wholemeal flour
1 oz (25 g) peanuts, chopped

2 oz (50 g) olive oil
2 teaspoons (10 ml) sesame seeds
paprika

Mix the first four ingredients together. Use, and top with the seeds and paprika.

Fork suppers

Tuna gratin

This is good dish for main-course-only entertaining, especially at supper, and an apricot pilaff makes the ideal accompaniment. If a dessert is also required, caramellized fresh fruit or perhaps sticky fig loaf (served with the after-meal drink) would complement it well.

SERVES 2

8 oz (225 g) butter beans, soaked
1 lb (450 g) broccoli
6 oz (175 g) tuna fish, cooked (ideally
  fresh; otherwise canned, very
  well drained)
freshly ground black pepper
1 teaspoon (5 ml) dried tarragon

1 oz (25 g) polyunsaturated
  margarine
1 onion, finely chopped
3 oz (75 g) wholemeal flour
¾ pint (450 ml) low-fat skimmed
  milk
1 oz (25 g) low-fat Cheddar, grated

Cook the butter beans in boiling water for about 1 hour or until really soft. Drain. Steam the broccoli until just tender. Arrange in an ovenproof dish. Combine the beans with the flaked tuna. Add the pepper and tarragon.

Pile this mixture in the centre of the dish over the broccoli. Melt the margarine, add the onion and sauté until transparent. Add the flour and cook for 1 minute. Add the milk and make up as for white sauce. Pour over the tuna and broccoli mixture. Sprinkle with the cheese and bake at 400°F/200°C/Gas 6 for 20 minutes until golden and bubbling.

Lamb tagine

This Lebanese dish is ideal for informal suppers.

SERVES 4

1 lb (450 g) lean, boned lamb, cubed
2 onions, sliced
2 green peppers, de-seeded and sliced
½ head celery, chopped
1 tablespoon (15 ml) wholemeal flour
freshly ground black pepper
paprika
1 teaspoon (5 ml) ground ginger

1 teaspoon (5 ml) turmeric
½ pint (300 ml) stock (possibly made
*   from fruit juice or wine)*
4 oz (100 g) dried apricots, chopped,
*   soaked in the stock overnight*
1 large piece orange peel, cut into strips
2 teaspoons (10 ml) lemon juice

Brown the meat well in a non-stick pan. Add the onions and brown them. Add the other vegetables. Sprinkle with the flour, pepper and other spices. Stir in quickly and pour over the stock with the apricots. Add the orange peel and lemon juice. Cook in a casserole at 325°F/160°C/Gas 3 for 1½ hours. Serve with bulgar pilaff, or turn into a casserole already containing 3 oz (75 g) cooked flageolet beans and heat through. Serve accompanied by a green-bean pan-fry (below) or another green bean side dish.

Green-bean pan-fry

This can be served either as a vegetarian supper dish or as a substantial side dish accompanying a meat course.

SERVES 4

1 tablespoon (15 ml) olive oil
3 tablespoons (45 ml) sunflower seeds
1 onion
1 carrot
3 cloves garlic
4 tomatoes
1 level tablespoon (15 ml) cumin seeds

pinch sesame salt
freshly ground black pepper
4 tablespoons (60 ml) tomato juice
1 tablespoon (15 ml) tomato purée
1 lb (450 g) runner or Spanish green beans
3 oz (75 g) low-fat Cheddar, grated
1 oz (25 g) split almonds

Heat the oil in a large non-stick frying-pan and brown the sunflower seeds. Chop the onion, carrot and garlic together, using a food processor if available. Add to the browned seeds in the pan. Chop the tomatoes and add to the pan. Stir in the seasonings, tomato juice and purée. Mix well.

Top and tail the beans, cut into bite-sized pieces and cook quickly, barely covered with water, until the water has almost evaporated. Drain and add to the pan. Cover and simmer gently for about 20 minutes. Sprinkle the cheese and almonds on top and brown under the grill. Serve with herby, garlicky granary French stick.

Glossary

acorn squash Flattish, pale yellow vegetables of the marrow family. They have a scalloped edge which must be cut through when preparing.

agar-agar A colourful and transparent form of dry seaweed, with a high mineral content, which can be used as a vegetarian setting agent instead of gelatine.

arrowroot A flour with a high starch content which can be used as a thickening agent and as a glaze for flans.

asafoetida A pungent, sulphur-like powdered spice, available from Indian food shops. Use sparingly.

ascorbic acid Vitamin C.

barley A useful source of calcium. Use pot barley, not pearl, for wholefood recipes.

barley malt extract A natural sweetener made from sprouting barley.

biotin Vitamin H.

bran The outer coating of cereals. Wheat, oat, rice and soya bran are available from health-food shops.

brown rice Whole-grain, unrefined rice, with nutrients retained.

buckwheat High in protein, this grain can be used whole, like rice, or ground, like wheat flour.

bulgar (also known as cracked or crushed wheat) Wholewheat grains that have been parboiled, dried and roasted.

buttermilk This is skimmed milk with the addition of a culture. It is slightly acid in flavour. Use with muesli, in scones and as a drink with mineral water.

cardamom A pungent, aromatic spice invaluable in Indian cooking.

carob A broad bean-shaped pod of chocolate-like flavour, used in confectionery and sold as a powder for cooking. May be used as a direct substitute for chocolate or cocoa.

cod-liver oil A very rich source of the fat-soluble vitamins A and D believed to prevent hardening of the arteries.

coriander A leaf herb and seed spice. The leaves are flat and green; the seeds are round, pale brown and pungent, and can be used whole, crushed or ground.

cumin A seed spice that benefits from dry roasting. It may also be used ground.

fennel seeds Light brown, oval seeds used for their spicy licorice-type flavour.

five-spice powder (Chinese name: *wuxiang*) Available from Chinese food shops, this is a blend of star anise, cinnamon, fennel, cloves and Sichuan pepper. Use sparingly.

fructose Fruit sugar.

honey A natural sweetener composed of sucrose, water, glucose, fructose, dextrine, maltose and protein together with some vitamins and minerals.

kelp Powdered seaweed, rich in iodine. Available from health-food shops.

legume Any vegetable of the pea or bean family.

milk, skimmed Milk with the cream removed, which makes it lower in both fat content and calories than whole milk.

millet Yellow grain which is high in protein, calcium and lecithin but contains no gluten. Use in pilaff and similar dishes, as rice.

miso Japanese fermented bean paste used for flavouring and available from health-food and some oriental food shops.

monosodium glutamate (MSG) A flavour enhancer in the form of fine white crystals formed by acid hydrolysis of soya beans or other plants. Undesirable for people on low-sodium diets.

mustard oil A vegetable oil flavoured with mustard seeds, used in Indian cookery.

peanut butter The wholefood type does not contain sugar or other additives and can be bought from health-food stores.

seeds Pumpkin, sunflower, sesame, poppy and linseed are all good sources of fibre (pumpkin being particularly rich in zinc, sunflower in iron).

semolina Derived from whole wheat grains, this is used in particular for pasta.

sesame seed oil High in polyunsaturates, this is available as a cooking oil and also in a much darker version as a seasoning, which is rich, pungent and delicious.

sesame seed paste See *tahini*.

sesame seeds Small and egg-shaped, both cream and black seeds are available. Best roasted, they can be used in salads and toppings as well as in baked goods.

sesame seed salt This Japanese condiment, a mixture of sesame seeds and salt ground together, contains half as much sodium as regular table salt.

sprouting grains, etc. Most peas, beans, seeds and grains may be sprouted. The nutritional value of these foods increases dramatically in sprout form due to the chemical change that takes place.

skimmed milk See *milk*.

stock cubes, low-salt These are available from health-food shops.

sweet cecily A fern-like herb smelling a little of aniseed. Used with acid fruits such as rhubarb, gooseberries or apples it reduces the need for additional sweeteners.

tahini Sesame seed paste, from de-fatted sesame seeds, this paste can be used to thicken sauces and soups as well as in dips (including hummus) and pâtés. It is also useful for salad dressings and can be spread on bread.

tandoori paste The best varieties are Indian brands, but check the label for salt content.

tofu The Japanese name for beancurd, made from soya beans, high in protein, low in fat and excellent as a meat substitute.

tomato powder Available from health-food shops.

vegetable stock cubes These are available in low-salt varieties from health-food shops.

worcestershire sauce A low-salt version is available from health-food shops.

yeast spread Rather like vegetable extract but low in sodium and additive-free, this is sold in health-food stores.

Index

Acknowledgements

The author wishes to thank Sandra Grant, whose idea it was in the first place.

Some of the material in this book has previously appeared in *Healthy Living* and is reprinted here by permission of the publishers.